S0-BCV-747

The Book of Job Unfolded

William Henry Green

Revised and Edited by Michael J. McHugh

Copyright © 1996 by Christian Liberty Press

All rights reserved. No part of this book may be reproduced or transmitted in any form or by any means, electronic or mechanical, without written permission of the publisher. Brief quotations embodied in critical articles or reviews are permitted.

Christian Liberty Press
502 W. Euclid Avenue
Arlington Heights, IL 60004

Scripture references are conformed to The Holy Bible, New King James Version © 1982, Thomas Nelson, Inc., so that modern readers may gain greater comprehension of the Word of God.

ISBN 1-930092-03-2

Table of Contents

About the Author

William Henry Green was born in the year 1825 and died in 1900. He had the blessing of growing up in a strong Christian home with loving parents. By God's grace, little William professed Christ as his Lord and Savior at an early age.

After William Henry Green graduated from Lafayette College at age 16, he began to serve as a math tutor at his former college. He also began formal theological training at Easton Seminary, which lasted four years. After graduation from seminary, Mr. Green pastored the Central Presbyterian Church of Philadelphia until the year 1851.

Late in 1851, Rev. Green began to assume new duties as Professor of Biblical and Oriental Literature at Princeton Theological Seminary. He faithfully labored at this calling for nearly fifty years. During his career, William Henry Green had to spend a great deal of his time writing and speaking against the rising tide of theological liberalism at Princeton. The following book on the life of Job was one of the few books that Mr. Green wrote simply to expound the Scriptures, and not to answer Bible critics. Professor Green was not only a gifted writer but a first-class scholar. He was among the few professors at Princeton who was willing to stand openly and boldly for orthodox Bible doctrine.

The book that Mr. Green wrote on the life of Job was originally printed in 1873 as *The Argument of the Book of Job Unfolded.* The 1996 edition of this classic text is simply titled *The Book of Job Unfolded.*

Few Christian writers and professors throughout Church history have equaled the faithfulness and consistency of William Henry Green. The Lord gave him to the church, the Lord took him away, blessed be the name of the Lord.

About the Reviser

The 1996 edition of *The Book of Job Unfolded* was revised and edited by Michael J. McHugh. Mr. McHugh has worked in the field of Christian education for over eighteen years with the Christian Liberty Academy of Arlington Heights, Illinois. During his time with the Academy, he has worked as a teacher, administrator, and textbook author.

In addition to his educational activities, Michael McHugh has served as an elder at the Church of Christian Liberty in Arlington Heights, Illinois since 1993. Mr. McHugh resides in the Chicago area with his wife and five children.

Special Thanks

The publishers would like to acknowledge the fact that Mr. Peter Rubel provided many helpful comments during his review of the final draft of *The Book of Job Unfolded.*

Preface

The book that follows is designed to give Bible students a solid understanding of the major teachings of the book of Job. It is a general commentary on the primary lessons of Job and not a verse-by-verse study. Consequently, students are encouraged to read the entire story of Job directly from the Scriptures prior to beginning with their study of this book.

Unlike many modern newspapers, the following book has not been "dumbed-down" to a third or fourth grade reading level. The author and editor have endeavored to present readers with a rich and clear presentation of Job through the use of thought-provoking vocabulary terms. Serious Bible study students should strive to improve their Bible knowledge and vocabulary skills as they progress through their text.

Comprehension questions have been provided at the end of each chapter and a helpful outline is also printed at the back of the book. Students are encouraged to make use of these resources.

It should be noted that readers, who are not accustomed to dealing with the issues of sin and holiness on a serious level, will very likely have great difficulty in relating properly to the Book of Job. The spiritual struggles of Job can only be appreciated fully by those who are engaged in a personal commitment to fear God and keep His commandments. It is hoped that the following commentary will help to "revive" a genuine interest in the people of God to pursue personal holiness.

The book of Job teaches many important truths. One great truth found in this inspired text is that spiritual things are real. Life is not a mere physical phenomenon or material quest to survive. It is a glorious spiritual struggle. May the Lord Jesus Christ grant each person who studies this material a closer walk with Him.

Michael J. McHugh
1996

Introduction

The book of Job is not directly tied in with any other Scripture text and, therefore, can be understood on its own. We are sure that the book of Job was given by inspiration of God, though we are not certain who was the penman. The Jews, though separate from Job, because he was a stranger to the commonwealth of Israel, yet, as faithful conservators of the oracles of God committed to them, always retained this book in their sacred canon. The man, Job, is referred to by one apostle (James 5:11). Also, a passage from Job chapter 5:13 is quoted by another apostle, with the usual form of quoting scripture, *It is written,* I Cor. 3:19. It seems most probable that Elihu was the penman of it, at least of the discourses, because in (Job. 32:15, 16) he mingles the words of a historian with those of a disputant. If Job wrote it himself, then we might very well join some of the ancient Jewish writers who own him a prophet among the Gentiles.

It is, for the substance of it, a true history, and not fiction, though the dialogues are poetical. No doubt there was such a man as Job; the prophet Ezekiel names him with Noah and Daniel, Ezekiel 14:14. The narrative we have here of his prosperity and piety, his strange afflictions and exemplary patience, the substance of his conferences with his friends, and God's discourse with him out of the whirlwind, with his return to a prosperous condition, no doubt is exactly true. Nevertheless, the inspired writer of this book is allowed the usual liberty of putting the story of Job in his own personal style of writing.

The manuscript of Job is very ancient, though we cannot fix the precise time either when Job lived or when the book was written. So many, so evident are the marks of its antiquity, that we have reason to think that holy Job was contemporary with Isaac and Jacob; though not coheir with them of the promise of the earthly Canaan, yet a joint-expectant with them to the better country, that is the heavenly. Probably he was of the posterity of Nahor, Abraham's brother, whose first-born was Uz (Gen. 22:21), and in whose family religion was for some ages kept up, as recorded in Gen. 31:53. The land of Uz, where Job resided, is thought to be located in modern day Palestine.

In Job's time, God was called not only the God of Abraham, but the God of Nahor. Job lived while God was known by the name of God Almighty rather than by the name of Jehovah; for he is called Shaddai—the Almighty, above thirty times in this book. He lived while divine knowledge was primarily conveyed, not by writing, but by tradition; for to that appeals are here made, chapters 5:1, 8:8; 21:29; 15:18. And we have therefore reason to think that he lived before Moses, because there is no mention at all of the deliverance of Israel out of Egypt, or the giving of the law. We conclude therefore that this text dates back to the patriarchal age, and besides its authority, we receive this book with veneration for its antiquity.

This noble book presents to us, in very clear and lively characters, these four things among other:—(1) A monument of primitive theology. The early and great principles of eternal truth, on which true faith is founded, are here, in a warm and long and learned dispute. Were ever the being of God, his glorious attributes and perfections, his unsearchable wisdom, his irresistible power, his inconceivable glory, his inflexible justice, and his incontestable sovereignty, described with more clearness, fullness, reverence and divine eloquence, than in this book? The creation of the world, and the government of it, are here admirably described, not as matters of nice speculation, but as laying most powerful obligations upon us to fear and serve, to submit to and trust in our Creator. Moral good and evil, virtue and vice, were never drawn more clearly into focus (the beauty of the one and the deformity of the other) than in this book. The unavoidable rule of God's judgment is also plainly laid down. (2) It presents us with a specimen of Gentile piety. This great saint was out of the pale of the covenant, no Israelite, no proselyte, and yet none like him for uprightness. It was a truth therefore, before St. Peter perceived it, that in every nation he that fears God and works righteousness is accepted of him, Acts 10:35. There were children of God scattered abroad (John 11:52) besides the incorporated children of the kingdom, Matt 8:11, 12. (3) It presents us with an exposition of the book of Providence. The prosperity of the wicked and the afflictions of the righteous have always been considered as hard subjects. Nevertheless, they are here expounded, and reconciled with the divine wisdom, purity, and goodness. (4) It presents us with a great example of patience and close adherence to God in the midst of tremendous hardships. Upon the whole, we learn that many are the afflictions of the righteous but that the Lord delivers them out of them all.

The book of Job follows this basic order:

1.   The history of Job's sufferings, and his patience in dealing with them (Chapters 1 and 2), not without a mixture of human frailty (Chapter 3)

2.   A lengthy dispute and debate between Job and his three friends, Eliphaz, Bildad, and Zophar regarding his innocence or guilt (Chapters 4-31)

3.   Two moderators enter the discussion, first Elihu (Chapters 32-37) and then God himself (Chapters 38-41)

4.   Job repents of his folly and prays for God to forgive him and his three friends. God accepts Job's repentance and prayers and restores Job's former prosperity two-fold. (Chapter 42)

Walking by Faith

If, on a quiet sea,

    Tow'rd heaven we calmly sail,

With grateful hearts, O God, to thee,

    We'll own the fav'ring gale.

But should the surges rise,

    And rest delay to come,

Blest be the sorrow, kind the storm,

    Which drives us nearer home.

Soon shall our doubts and fears

    All yield to thy control:

Thy tender mercies shall illume

    The midnight of the soul.

Teach us, in every state,

    To make thy will our own;

And when the joys of sense depart,

    To live by faith alone.

Chapter 1

Job's Happy Condition

"There was a man in the land of Uz, whose name was Job; and that man was blameless (perfect) and upright ..." (Job 1:1)

The book of Job is one of the most remarkable in the Old Testament. Apart from its inspiration, and considered simply as a literary production, it bears the stamp of uncommon genius. It is occupied with a profound and difficult theme, the mystery of divine providence in the sufferings of good men. This is not treated in the abstract, in simple prose or in a plain didactic method. But an actual case is set vividly before the reader, in which the difficulty appears in its most extreme form. By an extraordinary accumulation of disasters a man of extraordinary piety is suddenly cast down from his prosperity, and reduced to the most pitiable and distressed condition. And then there is unfolded in the most masterly manner the impression made on others by the spectacle of these calamities, as well as the inward conflict stirred in the sufferer himself. We see Job's bewilderment and sore distress, his alternations of despair and hope, his piteous pleas for a sympathy which is denied him and his irritation under the unjust suspicions which are cast upon him, his wild and almost passionate complaints against the Providence which crushes him, intermingled with expressions of strong confidence in God which he cannot abandon. This wild tumult in his soul is graphically depicted in its successive stages, until we are brought to the final solution of the whole, and the vindication at once of the Providence of God and of His suffering servant. And all this is set forth in the loftiest style of poetry, abounding in fine imagery and containing passages of deep compassion as well as of rare nobility and power.

The book of Job well deserves the mountains of acclaim which have been bestowed upon it as a product of the poetic art. And while we humbly receive its inspired lessons, there is no reason why we should be insensible to its other attractions. The Bible is not, indeed, amenable to the laws of criticism, nor to be judged by ordinary standards of taste. When God speaks to us, we must reverently listen and obey, however homely the medium through which He communicates His will.

Nevertheless, we should stand in wonder of this holy book, and to its adaptation to the needs of all classes of people during all times in history. Like the inexhaustible supplies of Nature in its manifold diversity, the volume of divine revelation gives us not only the massive granite and the ponderous metal, but the sparkling and polished gems of thought; not only the basic articles of food, but the rarer delicacies. So it is that the poetic genius is graciously spread throughout the sacred scriptures in the sweet lyrics of David, the impassioned fire of Isaiah, and the marvelous beauty of the book of Job.

The principal personage of this book, and the one about whom the interest chiefly centers, is Job himself, a venerable and patriarchal character, whose fortunes are detailed to us at an important crisis in his life. Some have thought that he was not a real, historical person, and that the narrative of the book is not one of events which actually took place, but that it is rather a fiction or a parable like that of the Prodigal Son or the good Samaritan. Such people believe that the book of Job is designed to represent not some one person to whom all this happened precisely as is here detailed, but a whole class, such as is often met with in real life. This, however, cannot have been the case. It is related not as a parable, but as a history, instructive throughout, as all the Bible histories are, but still an actual, veritable occurrence. And Job is spoken of in other parts of Scripture as a real person, and in connection with other real persons like Noah and Daniel, and the events of his life are referred to in a manner which strongly implies that they had actually occurred (Ezekiel 14:14). We can have no doubt, therefore, that, with all the poetic embellishment of the narrative, Job did actually live, and the history took place as it is here related.

At this point, we will proceed to consider the life of Job. We will consider his character and condition when he is first introduced to our notice, his great excellence and piety and his happy, prosperous state. These important issues are sketched briefly, but strongly, in the opening verses of the first chapter, and again in chapter twenty-nine, where, after his gloomy reverses, Job pathetically recalls the joys of former years.

We commonly think of Job as a sufferer; and the lessons that we most associate with him are those which concern affliction. His great sorrows form indeed the grand crisis of his life; and it is to their exhibition, together with the attendant principles of the divine administration, that this book is chiefly devoted. But the very point of the whole lies in their exceptional character, which requires an explanation. If this were not so, there would be no mystery to be explained. The enigma is in the contrast between what Job had to endure and what was in fact his ordinary experience up to the time when he was overtaken by these extraordinary calamities. *"...godliness is profitable for all things, having promise of the life that now is and of that to come"* (1 Tim. 4:8) This was fulfilled in the life of Job up to the time of his heavy trial, which had been one continued course of prosperity and happiness. It seemed as though nothing were left him to desire. As he himself expresses: *"In the days when God watched over me, When His lamp shone upon my head.... When my steps were bathed with cream, And the rock poured out rivers of oil for me! ... My root is spread out to the waters, And the dew lies all night on my branch."* The freshness of a well watered tree, the richness of butter and oil, the brilliancy of God's own light, are the figures which set forth his joyful and prosperous abundance. And, as the tempter sneeringly said, Job had not feared God for naught. God has made an hedge about him and about his house and about all that he had on every side. He had blessed the work of his hands, and his substance was increased in the land.

While, therefore, we go very properly to Job's dark hours to learn the uses of affliction, and all the salutary lessons which accompany it, it behooves us likewise to remember the lesson of all those years of blessings. God's blessing attends the righteous. *"... He who would love life And see good days, Let him refrain his tongue from evil, And his lips from speaking guile; Let him turn away from evil and do good; Let him seek peace and pursue it. For the eyes of the LORD are on the righteous, And his ears are open to their prayers; But the face of the LORD is against those who do evil"* (I Pet. 3:10-12).

Let us never neglect to consider the piety and the happy estate of Job, with the view of taking note how these are combined in the ordinary providence of God. The Bible does not indicate that there are no exceptions. There are such exceptions. There are grave and weighty reasons why there should be. Job himself was a notable exception at one period in his life. In considering the number and the mystery of the exceptions we must not forget the rule, a rule verified for the most part even in the general tenor of the lives of those who constitute the most notable exceptions. Happiness and godliness go hand-in-hand in the ordinary experiences of this world.

Let us consider at this point, the simple description here given of the godly character of Job. He is evidently portrayed as a model man. God Himself says of him, "There is none like him in the earth." And in the delineation of Job's piety, notice, first, two negative particulars, two

3

omissions in the narrative, which are highly significant, especially as found in a book belonging to the Old Testament.

The first is that no account is made of ancestry or of connection with the covenant people of God. There is no mention of Job's parentage, no hint of his relationship to Abraham. He was plainly not one of his descendants. Now if what secures the favor of God be a pious ancestry, or a connection with the outward visible Church, it is unaccountable that in the case of Job, held up as a model before all ages and generations, and of whom God gives such a testimony as he does of no other, that these things are not so much as once alluded to, even for the sake of explaining their absence or omission. Evidently it is not outward associations or connections, though of the most sacred kind, that constitute the evidence and pledge of God's favor, but personal character and life. In every nation and in every community, he that feareth God and worketh righteousness is accepted of Him. The important question is not, Are you a Jew or a Gentile? Are you a member of this or that particular branch of God's visible Church? Nor even, Are you a member of any outward body of professing Christians whatever? But, have you personally that character which is acceptable to God, and are you leading a life that is pleasing in His sight?

A second omission in the account of Job's piety, similarly significant, is that it is not described as consisting of ceremonial observances. No mention is made of any round of ritual service, no fasts or purifications or tithes, no rigorous periods of abstinence or self mortification. We notice no priestly intervention, no holy order of men through whom grace was dispensed as its sole appointed channel. The only religious rite referred to is the simple sacrificial worship of patriarchal times, maintained by faith in the sacrifice and the atonement that was to come, and which was afterwards accomplished by the Son of God on Calvary. Job was a priest in his own house; his own hands offered the sacrifice. Though devoid of the grace of priestly consecration, it was accepted. Job's religion was one of the heart and of the life, not of ritualistic service.

And it is the more striking because this is a model of piety belonging to the Old Testament. It is another illustration of the pains that were taken, even under that restricted and legal economy, to fortify the people against that spirit of bigotry and Phariseeism into which they were so prone to fall, and did fall, and which has in fact been the bane of vital religion in every age. Here was an outstanding and shining example. Job was an eminent saint of God, though his line of descent was not counted from Abraham, and though he did not practice the multiplied rites of the Mosaic ceremonial. Whatever advantages there are in an outward connection with the people of God or the visible Church, and whatever benefit may arise from outward attendance upon the services of religion,—and certainly neither of these are to be decried or undervalued, these connections alone will not win the approval of God. It is not critical that we be identified with Abraham's genealogy, but we must have a heart that loves to do the works of Abraham (John 8:39).

The general description of Job's piety is given briefly and simply in four particulars: he was blameless (perfect) and upright, and one that feared God, and shunned evil. But this statement, brief as it is, is very comprehensive. "He was blameless and upright." Uprightness denotes, in the first place, sincerity and straightforwardness. There was no double dealing or duplicity, no hypocritical pretense with Job, either towards God or man. He was sincere in his professions and honest in his practice. Uprightness, moreover, means conformity to the standard of right, and this both inwardly and outwardly. We read both of the upright in heart and of the man that is upright in his way. He was a man of integrity, therefore, both in spirit and in life,—a man attentive to his obligations both to God and man, and who punctually discharged them. And, with all, he was blameless and upright. Blameless, not of course in the sense that he was without sin. It is understood that according to the uniform teaching of Scripture, and the universal experience of men, perfection is unattainable in this life. Not that he was absolutely faultless, for there is no man that liveth and sinneth not. Job never claims spotless innocence. He himself says, *"Why then, do You not pardon my transgressions, And take away my iniquity? ..."* (Job 7:21a). *"...Though I were blameless, it would prove me perverse"* (Job 9:20). But he was perfect in the sense of completeness. His uprightness was not of that partial, limited kind, which restricts itself to certain classes of duties, while neglecting others; or confines itself to special times and occasions, while at others it is laid aside; which is very zealous about some of the commandments, to the disregard of others. Job was not like some men who can be devout in church and dishonest in their business, penitently ask God's forgiveness and yet be unforgiving themselves, who can profess great love to the Savior and yet be heartless to Christ's needy poor. He was blameless as well as upright. There was a completeness in his service to God. Job truly loved his Maker with all of his heart, soul, mind and strength.

5

And the spring of this blameless character and uprightness, or this complete integrity, was that he feared God. He set the will of God before him as his rule, the glory of God as his end, the approbation of God as his highest reward. In this pious fear of God he walked all the day long. This was his grand motive, overpowering everything else. This closed his ear against the siren song of temptation. This shut his eyes to every gilded lure of sin. The one thought, "Thou God seest me," was his safeguard and his stimulus. This impelled him to prompt and ready obedience to every divine command. This made him steadfast in his uprightness, and led to his perfectness and completeness in it.

It also led to the deliberate avoidance of a careless attitude toward sin, which is the finishing stroke to this description of a well-regulated piety. He "shunned evil": he carefully shunned all sin, kept aloof from everything that was wrong in heart, speech, and behavior. Some eminently good and holy men have great blemishes; they apparently lay out all their strength on the positive side of religion, and neglect its negative; they endeavor strenuously to do right, and forget to strive against doing wrong. And thus they leave the final side of the Christian character unfinished: the last side, which completes the whole, and gives it symmetry, is never added. A great gap is left unfilled. There was no such lamentable deficiency in the case of Job. *"He was blameless and upright, and one who feared God and shunned evil."*

Besides this general description of Job's pious integrity, two special traits are incidentally mentioned in different parts of the book, by which he was particularly characterized—not as though these were by any means the only ways in which his piety manifested itself. But they were marked and prominent, and they may serve as illustrations of his habitual piety and consistency in two separate spheres—home and abroad. In regard to the former, mention is made of a fact which serves to show Job's pious regard for the spiritual welfare of his children. It was the sacred habit of the family to throw the safeguards of religion around every period of mutual entertainment and social enjoyment. Whenever his children gathered, as they did regularly, at each other's houses on festive occasions, cementing and displaying their fond fraternal affection, it was Job's invariable custom to summon all together afterwards, and sanctify them, and offer burnt offerings according to the number of them all. For Job said, *"It may be that my sons have sinned and cursed God in their hearts"* (Job 1:5). "Cursed God" is too strong an expression for the meaning intended here. It is not blasphemy, or defiance of God, or malignant hatred of His service that he feared. The word is properly a formula of blessing, used in taking

6

leave of friends. It is commonly translated "bless" and is the same that is employed where it is said, *"And Laban kissed his sons and daughters and blessed them... and departed...."* (Gen. 31:55) *"So Joshua blessed them and sent them away"* (Josh 22:6); that is, he took leave of them, he said farewell to them, he bid them adieu. Job was afraid that his sons might have said farewell to God in their hearts; that they might have taken leave of Him; that in their thoughtless hilarity, they might have forgotten God and His presence, and acted as though they were out of his sight. He recalls them to solemn thought and to their sins by the offering of sacrifices according to the number of them all.

Job's piety manifested itself at home in thoughtful care for his children's spiritual good. But it was not limited to his own household. He sought the good of all. And he was especially forward in the relief of the needy and the protection of the injured. *"When the ear heard,"* he says, *"then it blessed me, And when the eye saw, then it approved me; Because I delivered the poor who cried out, And the fatherless and he who had no helper. The blessing of perishing man came upon me, And I caused the widow's heart to sing for joy... I was eyes to the blind, And I was feet to the lame. I was a father to the poor, And ... I broke the fangs of the wicked, And plucked the victim from his teeth"* (Job 29:11-13, 15-17).

We are further told that Job's outward lot was as happy as his character was exemplary. God's blessing was in the most marked manner bestowed upon his faithful servant, bringing him the most distinguished prosperity. He was happy in his family, having seven sons and three daughters, who were all settled near each other, and near their paternal home, and lived in the most delightful harmony. He had large possessions: his wealth in flocks and herds is recited, and it is added that he was the greatest of all the men of the East. And he was treated with the utmost respect by all classes, and held in the highest esteem. He says in his retrospect of these happy days: *"When I went out to the gate by the city, When I took my seat in the open square, The young men saw me and hid, And the aged arose and stood; The princes refrained from talking, And put their hand on their mouth;... I chose the way for them, and sat as chief; So I dwelt as a king in the army..."* (Job 29:7-9, 25). There seemed to be nothing to be denied in the way of worldly prosperity or earthly joy, beyond what he possessed.

Our thoughts are turned so frequently to the discipline of affliction and the spiritual profit which arises out of it, that we are in some danger, perhaps, of losing sight of the rule in the prominence which is given to the exception. And yet godliness has its temporal as well as its eternal rewards. The blessing of God attends the good, even in this present life and in regard to their worldly estate. There are promises of long life and prosperity, as far as it shall serve for God's glory, and their own good, to all those that keep His commandments. *"Blessed is every one who fears the Lord, who walks in His ways. When you eat the labor of your hands, You shall be happy, and it shall be well with you."* *"Evil doers shall be cut off: but those who wait upon the Lord, they shall inherit the earth."* *"Verily there is a reward for the righteous: verily he is a God that judges in the earth."*

It is true that worldly possessions bring a snare. And our Savior said that it is a hard thing for them that have riches to enter into the kingdom of God. And an apostle adds, Not many wise men after the flesh, not many mighty, not many noble, are called. So likewise another apostle: Hath not God chosen the poor of this world, rich in faith, and heirs of the kingdom? There is a peril, no doubt, in having a large share of this world's good. The danger is of cleaving to the world unduly, and of setting the affections upon earthly comforts and earthly pleasures, of being content with an earthly portion and ceasing to strive after or long for one that is heavenly. If the heart is given in idolatry to the world, and worldly objects become our end and aim, then we are worldly-minded and are not the servants of God. If any man love the world, the love of the Father is not in him. Ye cannot serve God and Mammon. They that will be rich, i.e.., that seek riches as their chief good, and make this their main, controlling object of pursuit, fall into temptation and a snare, and into many foolish and hurtful lusts, which drown men in destruction and perdition. The love of money is the root of all evil. Our Savior's rule is, seek first the kingdom of God and His righteousness,—first in order of time, first in importance, first in the urgency of desire and in the strenuousness of endeavor,—and all other things shall be added unto you (Matt. 6:33).

If this true order is preserved, then other things may be safely added, and no harm will result. The damage arises from the prevailing disposition to invert this order, to seek, the world first, and then as much of heaven as can be had without too great a sacrifice of worldly interests. Now upon the basis both of Scriptural teaching and of the common experience of men, it may confidently be affirmed that the true way to a happy life, even in this world, is found in the service of God. Our Savior announced the universal law when he said, *"He who finds his life will lose it, and he who loses his life for My sake will find it"* (Matt. 10:39). This is a seeming paradox, but it is perpetually verified. He who aims at worldly good fails to attain it. He either is unable to acquire that form of worldly good which he seeks, or, if he gets possession of it, he does not find it what he expected: it proves to be empty and insubstantial, and does not yield the satisfaction which he anticipated and desired. But he who abandons this world as his object, and aims at God's glory instead, gains that and this world too. It is as in the case of Solomon, who prayed not for riches, nor for long life, but for wisdom. God answered his prayer and then some. He gave him wisdom, and added long life and riches besides. Selfishness defeats itself: in grasping with eagerness after earthly good, it snatches a painted bubble, which bursts in its hands. Our truest welfare and highest happiness, even if we limit our view to the present life, will be most effectually secured by faithfully serving God and doing His will. It has passed into a proverb that honesty is the best policy. In a like sense and with similar limitations it is equally true that piety is the best policy. He who refuses to defraud his neighbor, not from any principle of integrity, but simply because he will thus in the end enhance his gains, does not deserve the praise of real honesty. And he who adopts the guise of piety to further worldly ends forfeits alike the smiles of God and the esteem of men. Nevertheless, goodness has its temporal rewards. Length of days is in Wisdom's right hand, and in her left riches and honor (Prov. 3:16).

That this is so in the general, and in its application to communities and masses of men, is obvious upon its simple statement.

Biblical Christianity fosters those qualities and habits which tend to worldly prosperity and success and to the promotion of the general good. It encourages industry, thrift, and frugality, and thus tends toward progress. On the other hand, it represses all those forms of vicious indulgence which lead to foolish occupation, and wastefulness. A large part of the extreme poverty and suffering that is found in the world is either directly or indirectly the consequence of criminal or vicious conduct, its natural and inevitable retribution affecting the vicious themselves or those connected with them. And it is not the evils of intense poverty alone that arise in this way, but miseries that affect wealthier classes, withering every joy, and souring all their possessions. God has set the brand of his disapproval upon sin by establishing moral consequences, which he has fixed in the world and by which a penalty has been fastened to transgression. These consequences can only be averted by turning away from the paths of evil in favor of the Word of God, which is the Word of Life.

Another fertile cause of suffering and sorrow in the world, which the prevalence of true Christianity would obliterate, is the injustice and unkindness of man to his fellowman. The strong oppress the weak, and they who cannot defend themselves are mercilessly trodden in the dust. *"...Men loved darkness rather than light, because their deeds were evil"* (John 3:19). Consequently, men engage in oppression and wars, with all the sorrows they occasion and the miseries they entail. How would the world blossom like an Eden, if God's Law held full sway, and its golden rule were enshrined in every heart and acted out in every life!

The Word of God is the only salt which can preserve from national corruption and decay. The history of the past utters its warning voice, showing how the downfall of nations swiftly follows on the heels of national prosperity, and the seeds of dissolution are involved in the very materials of their greatness and splendor. Accumulation multiplies the opportunity and the facilities of indulgence, and public virtue gives way, amid the glittering prizes held out for its allurement. Recent events have suggested gloomy thoughts to many thinking people in our country. Can virtue and integrity be maintained in our rulers and among our people, amidst the manifold temptations which are now assailing them, and before which many once trusted and confided in have sadly fallen? If honesty and integrity fail us in the centers of authority, if the enactment and administration of law can be tampered with by corrupting influences, and the public conscience becomes itself debauched by the corruption that is coming in like a flood, what must every sane mind anticipate as the inevitable result? In light of the growing and rapid-decay of virtue and integrity in legislative halls, in many of our courts of justice, and in leading financial circles, the most enormous evils are now opening before us. Can they be averted? The answer to this question depends upon another. Have we vital Christianity enough among us to check the progress of moral decay? Is there that fear of God and love of truth and right among our countrymen, which will insist on honesty and integrity in the administration of public affairs and in the conduct of moneyed corporations and commercial enterprises? The religion of the gospel is the stronghold of our national safety and of the perpetuity of our institutions. The more thoroughly this gospel shall leaven our people, the stronger we shall be, the firmer will be the pillars of our national prosperity, and the more abundant and widely diffused will be the blessings enjoyed by all our population. Blessed is that nation whose God is the Lord!

But the temporal blessedness springing from true religion has its application to individuals as well as to communities and masses. Communities are made up of individuals, and what tends to promote the welfare of the whole will often, in the same ratio, be conducive to the good of its constituent members. Upon this there is no need to dwell; but there are other considerations, which should likewise be taken into the account.

Happiness is not so dependent on external circumstances as many suppose. It is far more powerfully affected by men's own character and disposition. It lies not so much in the abundance of outward sources of enjoyment as in the capacity to enjoy. It is not secured by wealth, or social position, or success in worldly schemes. They who look at the bare outside of things are often grievously mistaken in their judgments. A splendid mansion may be the home of misery and care. And he who reclines on the most luxurious couch may be a stranger to peaceful rest. When we speak of the blessing of God accompanying fidelity to His service, we do not mean that the godly man will always be rich, or that he will always attain distinction, or that he will be invariably successful in his worldly schemes. But we say that while in ordinary cases he will not be damaged, but rather furthered, even in outward prosperity, by his faith, his real substantial happiness will be vastly promoted. He will the better enjoy what he does possess, he will draw a livelier and purer satisfaction from it, than if he had not the love of God in his heart and the fear of God before his eyes. If his religion has simply taught him this one lesson, in whatsoever state he is, therewith to be content, it has done much to establish and confirm his earthly happiness. For *"godliness with contentment is great gain"* (1 Tim. 6:6). It frees him from the dominion of evil passions, envy, jealousy, hatred, and the like, which are a fruitful source of discontent. It relieves him from the galling slavery of those in haste to be rich, with its attendant cares, anxieties, and consuming toil. It leads him to see in his earthly lot the appointment of his Heavenly Father, and thus cures him of all restless endeavors to overleap bounds he cannot pass. It gives him the consciousness of being at peace with his Maker and with all the world. He has the joy which flows from doing right; and every outpouring of unselfish love, every exercise of pure affection, every act of generous kindness to the needy to which his religion prompts him, is a new source of pleasure. Furthermore, all this is in addition to the delight of communion with God, the exercising of his regenerated faculties, and the enjoyment which is inseparably linked with the Christian's duties and privileges and his glorious hopes. In short, all that is summed up in that insignificant phrase, *"the joy of the Holy Spirit,"* (1 Thes. 1:6) a *"joy inexpressible and full of glory"* (1 Peter 1:8).

If any man on earth should be a happy man, it is he who owns Jesus Christ as his Lord and Savior. Looking honestly at this present life, and at the sources of gratification which are opened before us here, the good man is most truly blessed. Christianity does not foster gloom. It is a perennial spring of cheerfulness and joy. It does not abridge the enjoyments of life; it multiplies and heightens them. And there is no step that any person can take, more fraught with blessing to himself in this world as well as in the next, than to embrace God as his Savior and his friend. Those individuals who continue to cling to this world as their source of joy will find emptiness in the end, for it is certain that we brought nothing into this world and we will carry nothing away. He is no fool who gives away what he cannot keep to gain what he cannot lose.

CHAPTER 1: COMPREHENSION QUESTIONS

Job's Happy Estate

1. What is the primary theme of the Book of Job in the estimation of the author?

2. Why did the author believe that God chose to have the Bible written with a wide variety of literary styles?

3. What two reasons did the text give to support the belief that the book of Job is a true story about a real person from history?

4. Why did the author believe that the book of Job was not actually undermining the teaching of Scripture that "Godliness is profitable"?

5. About how many years of happiness did Job enjoy before his difficult trial?

6. Why did the author believe that Job found favor in the eyes of God? Was it due to his bloodline or connection with Israel?

7. In what sense is it proper to say that Job was "blameless"?

8. How do we know that Job was a faithful father?

9. In what ways does the practice of true Christianity or godliness help people to live a prosperous life?

10. What did the author believe was the true secret to happiness?

11. Did the author believe that everyone who follows God faithfully has the right to expect that he will be wealthy and powerful in terms of this world's goods?

12. What did the author believe was the only successful way to stop the destructive consequences of moral decay and sin in the life of a nation?

13. Did this writer believe that the personal integrity and character of public leaders and politicians was an important concern? If so, why?

14. How do the statements of Job help to demonstrate the true meaning of contentment?

15. At the end of Job's first series of calamities, did he really have any choice other than to seek God? Read John 6:53-69 before you answer this question.

Chapter 2

Satan

Again there was a day when the sons of God came to present themselves before the Lord, and Satan came also among them to present himself before the Lord. Job 2:1.

We are now introduced to a scene in the invisible world of a most impressive and surprising character. The amazing spectacle is presented of the Prince of Darkness appearing in the presence of the Most High. He comes not hypocritically in the guise of an angel of light, but in his proper character, with the rest of God's servants, to offer his homage, to receive his commissions, to render his stated account of work done and service performed. This astonishing and unusual representation has led some to entertain the opinion that the Satan of the book of Job is a different being from the Satan of the later Scriptures. Else how could he have his place among the sons of God? How could he come with them at stated times to present himself before the Lord? How could this be said of the enemy of God and the adversary of all goodness? A deeper view of this passage, however, reveals the harmony between the character in which Satan appears here and that which he maintains throughout the rest of the Word of God. He is not a mere spy, traversing the earth and intent upon selecting out all that he can discover. He is the old spirit of malice and wickedness, aiming to pervert men from the right ways of the Lord, and to destroy all goodness as far as it is in his power. And there is a profound meaning in his appearing here among the sons of God before the Lord. It is designed to express his subordination and subjection to divine control. He cannot act freely and at his own discretion. He is not at liberty to pursue his mischievous designs to whatever extent he may choose. There is a superior restraint to which he is obliged to bow, a superior will that sets limits to his rage, and allows him even within these limits to act out his evil nature only for the sake of some divine end, which he is made to be instrumental in achieving. It is evil in the person of its arch-representative and head, subject to good and constrained to be its minister. It is Satan actually exhibited in the attitude of a servant of God, and made subservient to the discipline and training of his people.

Satan is the enemy of goodness and the archangel, and with the malice and subtlety of a fiend, he is intent on our destruction, and hesitates at nothing by which it can be accomplished. He pursues his mischievous designs with sleepless vigilance and untiring passion. Invisible to human eyes, he has all the advantage of secrecy. He has his tools and associates in vast numbers of spirits of wickedness, who acknowledge him as their head, and are animated with a rage and cunning similar to his own. Satan is also joined by wicked men who are led captive by him at his will; and even in saintly hands from whom no danger is suspected, and who little suspect that they are fulfilling the commission of the devil. He has a control over external nature and over the bodies of men which we have no means of estimating, but which can only be conjectured from such facts as the disasters he brought upon Job, and the maladies he caused in the time of our Lord. And, more than all, he has direct access to our souls: he can touch in some incomprehensible way the springs of feeling and conduct, and exert an influence over us, which it may well make us shudder to think of.

All this is terrible. It is a dreadful thing to have a constant consciousness of danger, and especially of unknown danger; to apprehend that a vicious and unscrupulous foe is seeking your life, and that he has woven his plot so stealthily that you know not when you are safe, nor whom to trust. Satan is a murderer of souls, not merely an assassin who can kill the body.

It is an awful thing to be exposed to his treacherous solicitations. To come under his power is to take hold of hell and darkness. It is to be alienated from God and to incur the sentence of everlasting death. To yield to him in ever so slight a degree is to contract untold guilt, to bring ourselves under the displeasure of God, and put all hope out of reach. And yet we have no might to stand up against him. Surely, if there is any petition that we offer in all sincerity and with agonizing fervency, it is that which our blessed Lord has taught us: "... *do not lead us into temptation, But deliver us from the evil one*" (Matt. 6:13).

And yet these temptations cannot be escaped. It may be said, in a sense which is in no danger of being misunderstood, that by an ordinance of God they belong to this present state. Jesus was tempted of the devil; and the disciple is not above his Lord. The members must be made like their head. Through much tribulation we must enter into the kingdom of God. Fightings and fears beset the passage to the crown. The peril is awful, but success is glorious. *"Blessed is the man who endures temptation; for when he has been proved, he will receive the crown of life …"* (James 1:12).

Before entering strictly upon the development of the teachings of Job, which is the chief design of this book, we will first devote a chapter to a preliminary inquiry of no small practical benefit. What is the design of God in subjecting his people to this terrible ordeal? What are the disciplinary ends of the temptations of Satan, and how may we best overcome them?

And to this we answer:

1.   They should drive us to take refuge in God. One grand aim of the earthly discipline of God's people, in all its parts, is to bring them to a closer acquaintance with Him and dependence upon Him. They are made to learn more and more of His fullness, and to draw from Him larger and richer supplies. All the disclosures of His grace and of His unbounded resources made in His Word are designed to bring them to Himself as to an overflowing fountain, that they may drink the water of life freely. But in order that they may be stimulated to avail themselves of these benefits, and not perish in sight of abundance, an inward appetite is necessary, a hungering and thirsting after God, a craving for those blessings which He has to bestow. And the more imperative and urgent the sense of need which is awakened, the louder will be the cry for help, and the more earnest the application for it.

Here precisely the temptations of the Evil One have their place in God's great scheme of training. Every instinct of self-preservation in a grace-filled soul should lead it to cry mightily unto God for His delivering aid. Every temptation is attended with an imminence of peril, which should startle us out of our security, and lead us to fly for safety to Him who alone can save. He who has any just sense of his own weakness and frailty, and of the frightful evil of sin, must be steadily relying upon an Almighty arm. Only an Almighty arm can guard us from the assaults of one who succeeded even in enticing angels to their fall, and prevailed over Adam and Eve in all the vigor of their early integrity. We shall prove an easy prey, unless One, stronger than the strong man armed, secures our rescue.

A proper sense of our peril will not only tend to establish the general conviction that in God alone is our help, but will, in addition, lead us to fasten upon those particular assurances and grounds of encouragement which are afforded by Him for every crisis. The knowledge of the vast power of our spiritual adversary will lead us to take refuge in the omnipotence of God, and to place a new value upon this glorious attribute. The almighty power of God is then no longer an abstraction to us, an intellectual conviction, but a present practical necessity; not a perfection which we distantly contemplate, but one by which we live and without which we perish. The dire necessity which drives us to the fount of life is, in its results, a tremendous blessing. And the temptation of Satan, which terrifies the soul out of all self-dependence and creature-dependence, and compels it to find refuge in an almighty Savior, has accomplished a gracious end.

And as with this, so with other perfections of the ever-blessed God, and with the precious promises of His Word, and with the merciful provisions of the covenant of grace, and with the priceless salvation of our Lord Jesus Christ. The tempted soul learns afresh how to prize them, and embrace them, and cling to them, and rest upon them, and live by them. To what can he have recourse for protection against the subtlety and craft of Satan but the infinite wisdom and knowledge of God? How his dread of the rage of Satan enhances to him the value of the love of God! His unseen approaches exalt in our esteem God's gracious omnipresence. His access to our minds and hearts can only be rendered harmless by the indwelling and illumination of the Holy Ghost. What new delight is awakened by the thought of God's providential control, when we remember that He who has set the seas in their place restrains the malice of Satan. The Lord does not permit him to overstep the limits which our Father's love has fixed, and will not allow His people to be tempted above that they are able to bear, or without providing a way of escape for them that they be not overcome thereby! And what completeness is imparted to Christ's redemption, when we see that He triumphed over Satan, bruised the serpent in the dust, and shall bruise him under His people's feet! With what new eagerness will these dreaded temptations compel us to look to the cross, which is the symbol and pledge of victory over the destroyer!

2.   The temptations of Satan fulfill the important purpose of training the believer in the duties and exercises of Christian warfare. The sacred Scriptures teach us that there was a providential design in leaving a remnant of the Canaanites in the land of Israel: namely, to teach succeeding generations of the people war. There is no teacher like necessity, and no training in the military art comparable to that enforced by actual hostilities.

What emphasis there is in that direction of the apostle, *"Put on the whole armor of God, that you may be able to stand against the wiles of the devil"* (Eph. 6:11). Life in a sinful world does not provide times of peace and security, but of deadly conflict. It will not do to remain defenseless, and no armor that is defective or incomplete will carry the faithful through the battles of life. And what a school for practice in all the measures of offense and defense is this contest for life or death with such a foe! It is said of a great master in the art of war, that he learned his skill in strategy entirely from the powerful and able leaders with whom he was forced to cope. The Christian, in his protracted and stubborn contest with the wiliest of all antagonists, cannot fail to make distinguished progress in spiritual generalship, as well as to develop the qualities of a good soldier of Jesus Christ.

Nothing is better adapted to call forth a manly vigor than the necessity of strenuous exertion. The struggles one must make, the endeavors one must put forth to resist temptation and to overcome the Evil One, react to the greatest advantage upon Christian character. The circumspection necessary to escape his insidious designs, the diligence of one who is obliged to be ever on his guard, the fixed determination of one who has set his face like a flint for the celestial city, and who has resolved that he will be true to his God and his Savior at all hazards, tend to elevate rapidly the standard of the inner life.

And these temptations exhibit grace as well as develop it. It can never be shown either to himself or to others what a man is until he is tried. The constancy of Job and the power of his faith could never have been made to appear so conspicuous, if it had not been for the severity of the test to which he was subjected. This lay not only in the accumulated sorrows by which he was so suddenly overwhelmed, but chiefly in the suggestions of the tempter, who was mercilessly goading him on to give up his confidence in God, and to renounce His service. It was these sore temptations, which tortured him almost to despair, and wrung from him those bitter wailings with which the book abounds. And yet in spite of all, out of the midst of the depths we hear Job utter in the very face of the tempter his unabated trust in God, *"I know that my Redeemer lives"* (Job 19:25).

3.   The temptations of Satan, if properly met, may be made a means of intensifying our hatred of sin. He who has barely escaped the fangs of a venomous reptile will ever after entertain a deeper hatred of it. Sin is in every temptation offered to our choice. But it need only be stripped of its disguises to present it in its repulsive and odious features,

18

and make us shrink with loathing from the contact. The very act of repelling it will cultivate a spiritual sensitiveness which can less and less tolerate its hateful presence.

4.   But, in the fourth place, observe that temptation may be an aid to self-knowledge. The germs of evil are often undeveloped in the heart, and the man himself never suspects their existence until under the influence of some sudden or strong temptation. It is like the searching tests of the assayer exposing the presence of alloy in what might easily have passed for sterling metal. In the Christian's daily battle with sin, he experiences humiliating discoveries of the strength of secret corruption and subdued propensities to evil, appetites which he supposed he had under control resuming the mastery in some fatal moment. It is of these moments that the feebleness of his resolutions, insincerity in motives, and utter helplessness is fully realized. If these discoveries serve to humble him in the dust, and bring him in penitent brokenness of heart to ask for pardoning mercy, and lead him to be more watchful against his besetting sins, the ends of divine grace in suffering him to be overtaken by this temptation will be answered.

WAS Job Actually Sinful?

It was thus with Job. God himself testified that there was none like him in the earth, a perfect and an upright man, that feared God, and shunned evil. And yet there was a leaven of corruption in his imperfectly sanctified nature, of which he was not aware, until by the terrible thrusts of Satan it was exposed. Underneath his really sincere piety there was a blemish of self-righteousness, which made him bitter under the reproaches of his friends, and which, in the awful darkness of his trials, led him even to the point of justifying himself rather than God. Brought at last to himself, and dismayed at the thought of what he had allowed himself to utter, he says, "I abhor myself, and repent in dust and ashes" (Job 42:6). The design of God in this severe but salutary discipline was accomplished. Job had been led to know himself better than he did before, and he was humbled by this knowledge. The evil which before lurked within him unsuspected was detected and renounced.

5.   A fifth gracious end, which temptations may be designed to accomplish, is to wean the heart from the love of this present world. It is sheer cowardice in a soldier to be forever whining about the dangers or hardships of the campaign, and petitioning for a release. And it would be reprehensible in the Christian to be constantly sighing for the coming rest, merely to escape the toil of laboring in his Master's service. But this error is far less common than the opposite extreme of clinging

unduly to this vain world, and having the affections too firmly rooted here. To counteract this dangerous tendency, measures must be employed to loosen this attachment, by making the world seem less desirable, and causing us to sigh for what is purer and better. The weariness induced by the incessant conflict between the flesh and the spirit often weighs heavily upon the soul. It is a hard thing to be constantly crucifying our corrupt nature. We are never able with safety to relax our vigilance or to desist from effort. And it is disheartening to find how slow is our progress towards the completed conquest, even if we advance at all; how often the ground which we seemed to have won is wrested from us, and foes that we thought slain rise again to their feet as powerful as before. All this, though it should not lead us to abandon the fight while the enemy is still in the field, would make the news of victory more welcome. It gives sweetness to the thought of a world where there shall be no more sin, and into which temptation cannot enter, where inbred lusts and native corruption shall be removed forever, and Satan shall at length have ceased to annoy. And this suggests the farther thought:

6.   That the future glory shall be heightened by the temptations of this present time, which have been bravely met and successfully resisted. It is not merely that the coming blessedness shall be an ample compensation for all that tempted souls can now endure, that the flood of joy shall swallow up all thought of present pains, and the light affliction, which is for a moment, shall be followed by a far more exceeding and eternal weight of glory. But this glory shall, in various ways, be directly enhanced by those temptations, in so far as they have not been criminally yielded to, but in the name of the Master stoutly repelled. And thus what Satan intended for your hurt shall be converted into a source of everlasting profit. The experience of rest shall be heightened by the contrast of the preceding toil and strife. If the reward, though wholly the gift of grace, is in proportion to the service done or the fidelity shown, duty resolutely performed in the face of temptations of the evil one will surely receive a special acknowledgment. The training given to the spiritual faculties in the exercises of the Christian warfare, the development and expansion thence resulting to the powers of the soul, bear directly on our capacity for bliss and holiness. They who have attained the highest measure of fitness thus for the enjoyments of heaven shall have the largest experience of its blessedness. And further, those who have been driven by the assaults of the adversary into the closest union with their covenant God, and the most entire dependence upon Him, shall for

this reason again partake most freely of those joys which flow from endless communion with the infinite source of all blessedness.

7.　　　Finally, the temptations of Satan redound to the glory of divine grace. It belongs to the magnificence of God's universal government that opposition and hostility, to whatever degree and from whatever quarter, instead of tending to thwart or retard His plans, invariably contribute to further and promote them. Satan forms no exception. This archfiend, with all his legions and the entire kingdom of evil which he instigates and controls, in spite of their gathered forces and formidable numbers, and subtle craft and hellish spite, is absolutely powerless to prevent or to retard the execution of the least of God's designs. An infant in the arms is no more capable of slowing the movement of the worlds than Satan is to inhibit the fulfillment of God's sovereign decrees.

And this absolute control is rendered more illustrious by the manner of its exercise. It is not by bringing the resources of omnipotence to overpower the devil and his crew, and to chain them in the awful prison-house prepared for them, so that, driven entirely away from the theater of His operations, they can no longer interfere with or obstruct them. On the contrary, Satan is allowed free range, as the prince of the power of the air. He has installed himself as the god of this world. He is busy with his plans and his combinations. They are laid with consummate skill, and he is working them with tremendous energy. He is laboring to undo the work of God, to defeat the atonement, to destroy souls whom Christ would save. But his machinations shall recoil upon himself. Do what he may, let him rage as he please, let him accomplish his worst, and he is after all only building up what in his blind fury and malice he is endeavoring to tear down. The decrees which he would frustrate embrace himself and all his hateful deeds, as agencies co-operating to their fulfillment. With all his hatred of God and spite against His people, he cannot emancipate himself from that sovereign control, which binds him to God's service. In all his blasphemous designs he is, in spite of himself doing the work of God. In his rebellious efforts to dethrone the Most High, he is actually paying Him submissive homage. In moving heaven and earth to accomplish the perdition of those whom Christ has ransomed, he is actually fitting them for glory. Fiend as he is, full of bitterness and malignity, and intent on every form of mischief, he is constrained to be that which he most hates—a servant to God. Like the sons of God who assemble in the presence of the Infinite Majesty to receive the commissions of the King of kings, prompt to do His bidding and to execute His will, Satan is, though most reluctantly, and in a different sense from them, yet as really and as truly, a ministering spirit sent forth to minister to them who shall be heirs of salvation.

But the enforced subordination of this spirit of malice and wickedness to the ends of divine mercy and grace is rendered yet more illustrious, both to the praise of God's glory and to Satan's everlasting shame and crushing defeat by another triumph. This is the immediate agency by which his subjugation is effected. The New Testament Scriptures tell us about a vision of war in heaven. Michael and his angels fought against the dragon; and the dragon fought, and his angels, and prevailed not. Neither was their place found any more in heaven. And the great dragon was cast out, and his angels were cast out with him. Here, though he was defeated, it was by an antagonist worthy to cope with him. The rival forces fairly matched his own; and, however disastrous his overthrow, there was no dishonor in falling by such hands.

But when, smarting under his defeat in heaven, he went to make war with them which keep the commandments of God, and have the testimony of Jesus Christ, he engaged himself in a most shameful defeat. Whenever Satan, who aspired to be the leader of the host of heaven, and drew a third part of the angels in his fall, assaults the feeble children of men, he utterly fails to compass the ruin of one of them upon whom Jesus has set his love. He can terrify them; he can torture them; he can make them drag on the weary conflict with sin and corruption while life lasts; he can extort from them bitter groans of agonizing distress; he can shower upon them his fiery darts; but he cannot destroy them. Satan cannot by any means harm the feeblest of God's saints, who stands up against him in the name of the Lord. If he have on the armor with which divine grace has furnished him, and use aright the weapons with which he is supplied, and in humble dependence on his Lord abides faithful at his post, he is invincible; and the boastful foe, who came upon him ready to swallow him up, shall be driven back in shame and confusion. *"Resist the devil, and he will flee from you"* (James 4:7).

In the rapid view which has been taken of the subject, our attention has been confined to the temptations of Satan, as directed against the individual believer. Our limits will not allow us to extend our view to his assaults upon the kingdom of God in its collective capacity, and see how there, too, he most unwittingly acts under orders from the throne; how, in stirring up opposers to combat the truth of God, he but contributes to clear its statements, to unfold its richness, and render its defenses more impregnable. The gates of hell cannot prevail against the Church (Matt. 16:18). The earthquake, which in its violent upheaval threatens to demolish the city of God, but shows how absolutely secure its firm foundations are. He may shake earth and heaven, and the crash will only bring down what he had himself planned to build with rude untempered mortar, and it will only reveal in its unique stability, the immovable building of God.

And now in this warfare we are engaged. The temptations of Satan are not to be escaped: no sheltered position, no seclusion from the world, no sacredness of occupation, can screen us from them. The only question is, shall they prove our infinite damage, or shall they be made to recoil harmless and pointless? It is the most awful question which we can be summoned to answer; and yet the decision of this question may be said to have been placed by the infinite grace of God within our own control. If you yield to the tempter, you become his helpless prey. If you steadfastly resist him, confiding in the grace of God and the salvation of Jesus, he cannot touch a hair of your head. Temptation and sin, if you bravely resist them, will react to your everlasting welfare: your position is impregnable, the protection is ample, the armament is invincible, the supplies abundant, and the fortress can never be entered by the enemy, unless betrayed into his power by your own treacherous hands.

CHAPTER 2: COMPREHENSION QUESTIONS

Satan

1.   Why did the author believe that the Satan of the book of Job was the same Satan as presented elsewhere in Scripture?

2.   What other passage of Scripture, outside of the book of Job, speaks about an evil spirit coming before the Lord in heaven?

3.   In what sense is Satan a servant of God?

4.   Does man possess the power to defeat Satan's attacks in his own strength? Please explain your answer.

5.   What are some of God's purposes for temptation in the life of believers?

6. How does our faith in the power of God increase when we experience His acts of delivering us from sin?

7. In what sense is every believer at war with Satan?

8. What did the writer mean when he said that Job's trials put him in a type of spiritual "school"?

9. How does God use trials and temptations to wean our hearts from our love of this present world? Read 1 John 2:15-17 before you answer this question.

10. Read 2 Cor. 4:3-18. How do problems and temptations make us yearn for the glories that are in heaven?

11. Read Luke 12:13-31. How does this passage help us to understand how a true child of God could maintain his perspective on life while every possession is being stripped away?

Chapter 3

Job In Affliction

The Lord gave, and the Lord has taken away; Blessed be the name of the Lord. Job 1:21.

Shall we indeed accept good from God, and shall we not accept adversity? Job 2: 10.

We have seen Job in his piety and prosperous estate. We are now to see him in his sad poverty, and to witness his behavior in affliction. A change of circumstances often makes a great change in men themselves, or at least exposes a new and previously unsuspected side of their character, and develops unusual results. Sometimes it brings to light defects that had never been dreamed of in those who were esteemed almost faultless; sometimes it reveals unanticipated excellencies. Emergencies are the making of some men, and the destruction of others. The former rise in greatness, and in every noble quality of soul, in proportion to the increasing demands of the occasion. The latter are unable to abide the severity of the test applied to them, and fall before it. How will it be with Job?

A disclosure is made at the outset, to the readers of this book, of things that are concealed from the human actors in it. The veil that hides the unseen world is partially drawn aside, so as to afford us a glimpse of a spiritual agent, who is to give a new turn to events. The arch-enemy of man has had his eye upon Job. True to the instincts of his own vile nature, he has no faith in the reality of goodness. He sees in the piety of Job nothing but a refined form of selfishness. He serves God because it is in his interest to do so. God protects and blesses him, and as a matter of course he inclines to the quarter from which the favors come; but if these favors were to cease, the tempter urges, Job's piety would vanish with them. His goodness has its spring in its attendant rewards: withhold the latter, and Job will soon take leave of God and His service, which no longer yields him any advantage.

Satan is allowed to bring to an issue this question which he has raised. He may put Job's piety to the test, and in him he may test the question whether there is such a thing as real godliness in the earth, a godliness that is not merely self-seeking, but which heartily loves the right and cleaves to it, and chooses the service of God though no hope of profit may be forthcoming. Job is on trial, though he knows it not; and unfriendly eyes are eagerly watching for his stumbling. And he is on trial not merely for himself: the cause of religion is represented in him, the cause of God on earth, though he also is unconscious of the dignity of his position and of the importance of the battle he faces. Job is unaware that the eyes of the Lord are turned upon him with approval, and with a lively concern for the favorable outcome of the struggle in which he is engaged. Of the spiritual significance of this transaction, Job is profoundly ignorant. He feels the terrible pressure of his heavy sorrows, but he is not aware that they have been sent upon him as a test of character. He knows nothing of Satan's malicious designs, that center upon proving Job's love for God as a mere show. He knows nothing of the sovereign purpose of God, who means to establish its reality and power to the confusion of the tempter.

It is with trembling apprehension that we see such power granted to this unseen adversary, with liberty to use it against the unsuspecting patriarch: *"Behold, all that he has is in your power"*; *"Behold, he is in your hand"* (Job 1:12, 2:6). The contest seems fearfully unequal between this arch-fiend and mortal man, regardless of the sincerity and strength of Job's faith. It reassures us somewhat, however, when we observe that the tempter is, after all, limited and restrained by Job's almighty Guardian and Friend. The fiend cannot frame and carry out his wicked designs unchecked. He must have leave from the Most High before he can touch Job at all to harm him or lay his hand upon anything that he has. And, when permission is given, it is within fixed limits, which he may not overstep. When Job's property was put at Satan's disposal, it was with the accompanying restriction: *"Only do not lay a hand on his person"* (Job 1:12). When Job's own person was further subjected to his power, it was with the added requirement, "But spare his life." With all the limitations, however, a tremendous range was conceded to this enemy of all righteousness, and the assault which he makes is a frightful one. Can Job endure the shock?

In order that we may properly appreciate the conduct of Job in his affliction, we must further take into account another consideration. Job went into his trial destitute of many of those firm supports and grounds of consolation, which are now so plentifully supplied to suffering saints.

Those revelations had not yet been made, upon which the believer now so firmly rests his hope in times of deep distress. Truths, which are as familiar to us as household words in the gracious disclosures of the gospel, had never been clearly set before the minds of men. Perhaps it may be said that the faintest conceptions of them had scarcely dawned on any human consciousness. The king's broad highway through the wilderness of earthly sorrow, along which suffering pilgrims can now pass in comparative safety and comfort, had not then been constructed. Its route had not even been surveyed, not a pathway broken. Job was one of the hardy pioneers to whom this primary task was committed. He had to make his own way, without a visible guide or chart or knowledge of the ground. Job was, after all, unsheltered from the tempest and the storms, which broke over him without mercy. Prophecies yawned at his feet, swollen streams ran across his route, and there were treacherous bogs in which he might be hopelessly mired. It should not seem strange that Job's stout heart quailed at the terrors which surrounded him. Yet, in spite of all, he pushed his way through, and the path which he opened has defined the route for many travelers since. There is not a weary sufferer in Christendom who is not indebted to the patriarch of Uz, who has not been helped and aided by his example of faithfulness and undying hope. He grappled with the mystery of affliction in all its unexplained darkness and difficulty, and his discoveries have been the heritage of God's people ever since.

Think for a moment what it would be to encounter crushing sorrows not only without Calvary and Gethsemane and the sympathy of the incarnate Son of God, who is Himself touched with the feeling of our infirmities; but to go into trials that offer no bright spot this side of the grave, with no clear view of that eternal blessedness, in comparison with which all earthly sorrows, however grievous in themselves, and long continued, are nevertheless light and momentary. How would you function without solid assurance that present griefs and sufferings shall be overbalanced and outweighed by that far more exceeding and eternal weight of glory? What would it be to encounter frowning providences without the distinct understanding that these are nevertheless consistent with the abiding, unchanging love of our heavenly Father? Job had an understandably difficult time grasping that his trials were not tokens of God's displeasure. Only New Testament believers can easily see that trials are not evidences that He has withdrawn His love or has shut up His tender mercies. On the contrary, whom the Lord loveth He chasteneth. There is a paternal discipline in affliction. It has a gracious design, and will have a salutary result. The rod is in a loving Father's hand: its strokes are not capriciously nor unkindly given. They are administered solely for our good, for as the Apostle Paul explained, *"all things work together for good to those who love God ..."* (Rom. 8:28).

Deprive the sufferer of the comfort afforded by his knowledge of these precious truths, hide from him the benefit to be derived from affliction, take away his consciousness of the divine love in the midst of it all, and remove from Him the assurance of the everlasting reward which shall infinitely more than compensate all that he now endures, and how defenseless would he appear in the presence of heavy griefs? These wellsprings of consolation had not yet been opened. These comforting truths had probably never found utterance in human speech. Simple and obvious as they now appear to us from frequent repetition, and belonging to the very alphabet of our religion, they had never been distinctly formulated, and no clear conception of them had ever been reached. Job must fight the battle without the aids which his experience as well as later revelations have furnished us. His sorrows came upon him, not for his own sake merely, but for ours. A new lesson was to be given to the world; and Job was to be the point of instruction. The stream of adversity swells around him, until in danger of sinking he is compelled to struggle with all his might to get upon the sure foundation. Where he finds firm footing, other children of sorrow may safely tread.

The spectacle before us, then, is that of this eminent man of God, chosen to be the leader of the band of sufferers in their mortal conflict with evil and the evil one. He goes into the strife unpracticed and unawares. The onset of the foe is fierce and furious. Will even Job be able to stand in the evil day?

The conflict unfolds itself in three successive stages of growing violence, and the demeanor of this holy man is depicted to us in each. In the first, we behold him in one evil day suddenly and irretrievably stripped of all his possessions. In the morning his sky was without a cloud. He was in the midst of the prosperous abundance which he had long enjoyed, and seemed to have every reason to feel secure of its continuance. It was in fact a day of special festivity and family reunion; and, so far from leading to the anticipation of evil, it was an occasion of more than ordinary joy. Happy in his children, and in his possessions, and in the respect and consideration universally accorded to him, his cup of blessing overflowed. And there was nothing to suggest the likelihood of a coming storm. And yet, before that day was ended, everything was gone. To such destitution was he reduced that his condition is aptly likened to that of a newborn child. He came naked into the world; and now that he had been stripped of all, he shall leave it as naked as he came.

Suddenly, and without a moment's warning, the storm of calamity burst over the head of the doomed patriarch. One messenger of evil chased another with tidings of disaster. One had not ended his tale of loss before another came with a tale more difficult still. His oxen and his asses were driven off by the wild and roving tribe of the Sabeans; his sheep were consumed by fire from heaven; his camels were carried away by plundering bands of Chaldeans; and his servants put to the sword. And, to complete the dismal intelligence of woe, the house in which his children were assembled, and passing the hours in glad hilarity, was overturned by a tornado and fell upon them all, crushing them to death. In one moment of terrible trial the stricken patriarch has lost his children and his property. All is taken from him in an instant; and, of all that he had cherished and delighted in and prized of earthly good, he had nothing left.

If the calamity had been less sweeping and universal, it would not have been so overwhelming. If something had been spared him, if it had been only a part of his property and not the whole which was taken, the loss might still have been considerable, it might have been heavy, it might have involved the greater part of his fortune; still, if he had not lost all, it would have been easier to bear it with composure. Or though all his property were taken from him, if those possessions had been left which were dearer far than flocks and herds, those precious domestic treasures which he valued beyond all his wealth, if his beloved children had been spared, it would have been easier to bear the loss of all beside. It would have been hard to part with one of that cherished circle that he prized so much and loved so fondly; but all, and all at once, this was bereavement and desolation indeed.

If the blows had not fallen so suddenly and in such quick succession, if he could have had some time in which to steady himself for the shock, if there had been some intervals of relief in which he could have summoned all his strength to meet the coming blows, it would have seemed less dreadful, it would not have been so crushing as when the whole dire weight came down upon him at a stroke. By this accumulation of sorrows so suddenly sprung upon Job, the violence of the attack was increased to the utmost, and thus his steadfastness was put to the severest test. Can the tempter drive him thus to give up his integrity and abandon his trust in God?

Under the pressure of intense affliction men are in danger of falling into one of two opposite extremes, either of which is inconsistent with fidelity to the Lord's service. The first is that of repining and murmuring at the divine allotment. The other is that of bearing it in a spirit of hardened indifference. The wise man warns us against both. *"My son do not despise the chastening of the Lord, nor detest His correction; For whom the Lord loves He corrects ..."* (Prov. 3:11, 12). Job avoided both these dangers in that subdued but noble demeanor which has been in all ages since the model of submissive resignation. The stricken patriarch, bowed with grief, adopts the token of the most profound humiliation and sorrow: he rent his mantle, and shaved his head, and fell down upon the ground. Not to sit in sullen silence and brood despondently over the terrible losses which he had sustained, not to complain of the providence of God which had dealt so hardly with him, no, he prostrates himself in reverential worship; he bows with meek submission to Him who had smitten him, and his only language is that of grateful adoration to the Source of all blessings, who in removing all had but taken away what He Himself had given. Job fell down upon the ground and worshipped and said, *"Naked I came from my mother's womb, And naked shall I return there. The Lord gave, and the Lord has taken away; Blessed be the name of the Lord"* (Job 1:21). Can humble,

30

trustful piety reach a sublimer utterance than this? He has been cast down from the height of his prosperity, has suffered the total wreck of his fortune and the loss of all his family; he is burdened with his crushing sorrows. Nevertheless, with bleeding heart and prostrate form, this venerable man utters not one word of complaint. So far is he from giving up his confidence in the goodness of the Lord, that he strengthens himself in this confidence by the very greatness of the calamity that he has suffered. Job draws his argument of praise for the multitude of God's mercies from the very bitterness of the cup that is now pressed to his lips.

The submission of Job is not merely that he yields to what is inevitable, that seeing the stroke of fate has fallen, and its blow cannot be turned aside, and the past cannot be undone, he resigns himself to what is beyond the possibility of repair. Nor does he merely succumb to Omnipotence, convinced that it is futile to resist what the almighty God has appointed. None can stay His hand, or prevent the execution of His sovereign will. It can be of no avail to oppose his Maker, and so he subsides in forced acquiescence. Nor is it merely the rectitude of the infinite Ruler before which he falls prostrate, who has a right to do as He will with His own, and who can dispose of his creatures according to His sovereign pleasure. Job meekly bows not before the stroke of inevitable fate, not simply before the resistless energy of almighty power, nor simply before the righteous control of the sovereign Ruler, but before the goodness of the Lord, a sense of which now fills his heart proportioned to the magnitude of the loss which he has sustained. *"The Lord gave, and the Lord has taken away; Blessed be the name of the Lord"* (Job 1:21).The bitterness of his loss is made the measure of the preciousness of the blessings God had given. The severity of his trial consists in parting with what God had bestowed. Every pang that now rends his heart is a fresh proof of how gracious God has been. The magnitude of the loss determines the value of the gift, and the depth of his anguish enhances his grateful sense of the goodness of the Giver. The more deeply he mourns the treasures which have been taken away from him, the higher is his appreciation of the gracious kindness of Him who bestowed them. Thus the more profoundly he grieves, the more fervently he still blesses the name of the Lord.

Not that he sees the goodness of God in afflicting him for this was a lesson Job had not yet learned. The benefits and uses of affliction, and the gracious design with which it is sent of God, had not yet been revealed. It was through these trials of Job himself, and the disclosure of His purposes thus given, and the providential issue of His dealings with

His servant, that the first rays of light were shed on this dark and mysterious subject. It was partly in order to afford an occasion for giving these lessons to the world, which might lighten the sorrows, and ease the burdens, and mitigate the trials of subsequent sufferers, that these distresses were sent on Job. Thus did he in a measure suffer for our sakes, and by his stripes we are healed; as a forerunner and a type of the great Prince of sufferers, of whom this was true in its strictest and highest sense.

But these lessons, which we have learned from the example of Job and the measures of God's grace with him, as well as from later revelations, were all unknown as yet to the patriarch himself. He knew not that affliction was a means of grace, that there was healing in the bitter draught, that there was mercy in these seeming frowns, that all that he experienced was in fact the chastisement of love. He knew not even that it was a trial and a test of his integrity and pious faith in God nor that the Lord regarded with ultimate approval his steadfast endurance of the test thrust upon him by his great adversary.

And it heightens our conception of Job's sterling piety, and enhances to our view his sublimely meek and submissive demeanor, when we see him confronting the unsolved dilemma of this mysterious situation, by drawing from it fresh matter for grateful praise. He does not merely confess that He who gave might justly withdraw His own, so that, whatever his losses, his mouth is stopped from making any complaint. But the withdrawal of the gift makes him sensible of its greatness, and, instead of drawing from him the language of complaint, compels him to the utterance of praise, *"Blessed be the name of the Lord."*

The first stage of the trial is ended, and the tempter is foiled. The record is, *"In all this Job did not sin nor charge God with wrong"* (Job 1:22).

But the tempter is not yet satisfied, and Job's piety must be put to a yet further proof. He has properly accepted the loss of all outward possessions, the ruin of his property, the death of his children; but what if the blow should fall not on what he owns, but upon himself? Satan quickly plans a fresh onset, and leave is given him to aggravate the sorrows of Job, already so great, by an additional disaster. To the calamities previously sent is now added an infliction upon his own person, a most distressing, offensive, and acute disease, the symptoms of which was an eruption of painful ulcers covering his entire body. He was smitten with sore boils from the sole of his foot to his crown. *"And he took for himself a potsherd with which to scrape himself while he sat in the midst of the ashes"* (Job 2:8).

Can Job bear up under this new distress? What will be the effect of pain and bodily suffering added to the shock of former sorrows? Now that he is weakened by disease and distracted by torturing anguish in every member of his body, will it be strange if the trustful submission which he has maintained hitherto gives way? And though he has borne his previous trials with noble fortitude, could Job's piety be put to a test which it could not bear?

The trial proves too much for Job's wife. Her fortitude forsakes her at this new spectacle of woe. "Do you still hold to your integrity?" she says to him: "curse God," or rather, take leave of God, abandon his service, "and die." The wife of Job has often been misjudged, and the meaning of her words misunderstood. She has been censured as though she were destitute of piety, had neither love nor sympathy, for her husband, and were lacking, in fact, in common humanity. It has even been hinted that Satan showed his hostility to Job no less in sparing her to be a torment to him than in taking the lives of his children. The representation is frequently made that, never having sympathized with Job in his piety, she was provoked that he should maintain it still when it had proved so unprofitable and was so poorly rewarded. And she bids him curse God and die, as though she would have him bid defiance to his Maker, from whom he received nothing but unmeritted injuries and ill-treatment. Some also insist Job's wife was suggesting that he might as well die in the wretched condition in which he then was; it would the sooner end his misery and possibly also relieve her of her torment since he had ceased to be anything but a burden, of which she was willing to be freed.

We cannot but look upon this severity of judgment as quite undeserved. It is unfair to put the worst construction possible upon the language of Job's wife in this case, and then make her conduct on this occasion the measure to her whole life. Such a judgment is altogether misleading, and gives a perverted view of the incident itself which is here recorded, and of the design with which it is introduced. There is no evidence either here, or in the single allusion subsequently made to the wife of Job, 19:17, that there had been any unhappiness in Job's domestic life, or that his wife had been a thorn in his side, or anything other than the worthy partner of such a husband, his joy and solace. Furthermore, in the days of his former prosperity his quality of manhood could not have been as pure and untroubled as it is represented to have been, and when his prosperity again returns there is no intimation that she served in any way to make his happiness incomplete.

And, so far as appears, she had borne their first terrible trial with a like spirit of meek and submissive resignation to that of Job himself. She had faced adversity as bravely as he. At least we hear of no murmur from her lips any more than from his on that dreadful day of disaster and sudden shock, when property and children were all swept quickly away, and they were left destitute and alone. She offered no word of protest then, against Job's utterance of pious resignation. So far as appears, her heart went with his. She, too, parted with her wealth and with her children without complaining. How many women do you know today who could show such courage?

But when her last earthly prop is breaking, and her only surviving solace is perishing before her eyes, and she sees her husband in such misery and suffering, and sinking into death by so frightful a disease, she becomes frantic in her despair; her fortitude gives way; her trust in God, which she had cherished hitherto, passes under a cloud. She feels that it is a cruel turn of events, and He is cruel who has inflicted it. And she cannot bear to have her husband in his helpless misery continue to bless and to adore the God who is torturing him to death. A God so pitiless and so cruel it were better to take leave of than to worship. It were as well to curse Him as to bless, for in this desperate situation it can make matters no worse, for death is equally at hand in either case.

And thus the loving wife in the frenzy of her anguish has positioned herself unwittingly upon the tempter's side. It is not the first nor only time that fond hearts and friendly hands have unknowingly leagued themselves with the destroyer, and ignorantly done the work of Satan. That Job's wife did what she did under the impulse of her affections, seems to be implied in the connection. Her words are introduced as adding force to the temptation, and affording a fresh exhibition of the firmness of Job's piety. A cold, unfeeling sarcasm and a rude taunt from his wife would not have enticed Job to follow her advice. Instead of assailing his integrity at a new and tender point, it would have naturally thrown him into an attitude of resistance to the heartless and wicked suggestion.

But the case is altered, if we see in his wife one who tenderly loves him, and whom he fondly loves. She has stood firmly with him hitherto, but now at length her steadfastness is overcome. Job has borne all former disasters unmoved. His bodily sufferings do not even appear to shake his integrity. And now the solicitations of his wife he turns aside. His reply to her suggestion is not harsh and severe, as it is frequently interpreted, but rather the language of pained surprise. It is not a stern censure, but a mild rebuke, though certainly a clear rejection of her ill—judged counsel. He does not rudely charge her with being herself a foolish woman, whether the meaning be destitute of sense or lacking in true godliness. He simply says this was not spoken like herself; it is such a suggestion as he would not have expected from her. She had spoken not with her usual wisdom and pious feeling, but as one of the foolish women speaketh. *"What! shall we indeed accept good from God, and shall we not accept adversity?"* (Job 2:10)

Job's trust in the goodness of the Lord does not falter yet. Here was not, as in his former trial, a simple withdrawal of what God had previously given and in which the amount so withdrawn was simply an index to the goodness of Him who had bestowed it. There was now not the mere withholding of good, but the positive infliction of evil, of suffering and pain. Job knows not that this suffering contains a benefit, and is sent with a benevolent design. He cannot, therefore praise God for the suffering itself, and acknowledge in it a token of the divine goodness, as he might have done if the lesson had been taught him which the apostle expressed when he said, "We glory in tribulations also," "... *I take pleasure in infirmities, in reproaches, in needs, in persecutions, in distresses for Christ's sake*" (2 Cor. 12:9, 10). Job did not yet know that all things work together for good to them that love God. He did not understand that pain and suffering were or could be anything else but evils. Yet regarding them simply in this light, as evils, and evils received from the hand of God, they did not blind him to the fact of divine goodness and the great preponderance of blessing received from His bountiful hand. The evil does not by any means match the good, much less outweigh it. Shall we forget the immensity of the benefits bestowed because He also sends some suffering? Shall we receive good at the hand of God, and shall we not receive adversity?

Job is again victorious, and the tempter is once more foiled. His piety has proved equal to the severity of this fresh test to which it was subjected. "In all this," the record runs, "... *Job did not sin with his lips*" (Job 2:10).

But Job's trial is not yet ended. He has passed through two stages of it, and has successfully surmounted them. Thus far his piety has borne the test triumphantly, to the loss of his property and of his children with

35

noble resignation; with his heart wrung with grief, clad in the insignia of mourning and prostrate on the earth, he still blessed the name of the Lord. He bore the further infliction of what was deemed a fatal disease, accompanied by acute bodily suffering, with heroic fortitude; and though his wife herself threw her weight upon the side of temptation, he still held fast his integrity, and submissively received burdens as well as good from the hand of the Lord. But the third stage of the temptation is yet before him, and it will test his ability to endure suffering over a long period of time.

Many a fortress is secure against assault, which yet may be obliged to succumb to the slow and steady progress of a siege. Constant dropping wears away rocks. There are limits beyond which human endurance cannot go. The first onset of pain and suffering is not nearly so formidable as its protracted continuance, which wears out the strength and uses up the capacity of resistance. Pain which can be patiently borne for a short time becomes intolerable after a longer period. Sad indeed is the condition of the worn and weary sufferer, whose strength is exhausted, and hope pressed down. Such a person is unable to calm his irritated nerves or ease his aching limbs, restless through all the tedious night, and through all the day sighing for the night, though the night brings no peace. It is not so much the amount of pain endured at any one moment as its long and wearisome continuance that is so hard to bear. This weary, exhausting round of suffering, with no prospect of relief, is the third stage of Job's heavy trial. The tempter, who had twice failed in his fierce onset, would now wear him out, if possible, and break his strength by long-term harassment.

Day after day, week after week, he is still compelled to drag his heavy burden, and he does so in silence. How long we know not. It was some time after his seizure before his friends arrived to comfort him. Doubtless a number of days had passed before they heard of his calamity. A further interval was consumed in concerting an appointment to come. When they arrived, his disease had already so altered his features and form that they lifted up their eyes and knew him not. And after their arrival they sat with him seven days and seven nights before Job uttered a word of lamentation. Through all this protracted period he bore his grief in silence. But at length his sorrows grow beyond his power to suppress them, and he breaks forth in the piteous moanings of intolerable anguish. He has borne the torture with pious fortitude, until at length human frailty can hold out no more: he can endure it no longer, and he gives vent to the most distressed sighs and groans; but in it all observe that he does not rail against God.

In the most passionate manner he utters his wailing cry. With the most vehement expressions he heaps criticism on the day in which he was born; he wishes that day blotted from existence—in other words, that it had never been—so that it could not have inflicted upon him the misery of an intolerable existence. Oh that he had never been born! Oh that when born he had perished, neglected and uncared for, and thus might never have come to know the wretchedness of living! Oh if he had but found in early infancy a grave, which closes over all alike, and sweeps into its path the rich and great, kings and counselors, the master and his slave. Oh, how he longs for death! He would clutch at it as the miser grasps his gold, as men dig for hidden treasures. Why is this coveted privilege of death denied him?

Job the sufferer bemoans his dismal fate. It is the pitiful lament of one who has more laid upon him than he thinks he can bear. It is not the expression of considerate reflection. The sentences are not to be nicely weighed, and their propriety or impropriety passed upon as though they were spoken in moments of calm repose. They must be judged in reference to the humanity of Job. They are the language of one tortured beyond endurance, who cannot support the anguish that he suffers, and whose life has become an intolerable burden. Allowance must be made for realities of helpless, hopeless sorrow. His strength was not the strength of stones, nor his flesh of brass. While we do not seek to excuse Job's speech, we must try to understand and appreciate the fact that he is only a man. Job's comments only represent the bitterness of irrepressible woe.

Still, bruised as he is, hopeless of good, with but one wish, and this that he might die, Job does not reproach or revile his Maker. The tempter has broken his spirit, and crushed him to the earth; but he has not succeeded yet in wresting from him his integrity or bringing him to forsake his God.

Here we must leave the patriarch for the present. This third, most dreadful stage of his trial is not yet ended. The tempter has not relaxed his hold. He has new instruments of torture to apply to the victim already reduced to so pitiable a condition; and he will use them mercilessly. He sees his advantage in Job's extremity of misery, and he will push it to the bitter end, if so he can wring from him the renunciation of his trust in God. Will he be able to achieve his malicious design? The future will reveal. Meanwhile let it be recorded that he has not succeeded yet. In the desperate straits to which he has been driven, Job has not yet renounced the service of the Lord.

And may He whose grace supported Job in all his dreadful trials also grant the same grace to us—grace according to our need, grace to do according to the measure of the task required of us, grace to bear according to the measure of the burden laid upon us. Praise be to the God of all grace. Amen.

CHAPTER 3: COMPREHENSION QUESTIONS

Job In Affliction

1. In what way did Satan misjudge the motives of Job as he followed the Lord each day?

2. Did Job realize that he was in a special trial or contest with Satan?

3. What do you think about the statement, "Anyone can pretend to be the captain of a ship during calm weather, but only a true captain can weather the storms?" Relate this statement to Job.

4. What spiritual tools did Job lack during his trials as compared with those that are enjoyed by New Testament believers?

5. Briefly describe the major calamities that afflicted Job in chapter one.

6. Did the author believe that God had permitted Job to be afflicted for purposes that involved more than just Job himself? If so, what were some of the additional reasons?

7. What is the difference between toleration and submissiveness?

8. Was Job merely tolerant of God's will or was he truly submissive to the Lord's providence?

9. Why do you think Satan choose to harm Job in progressive stages rather than in one major attack?

10. What did the author believe was the reason why Job's wife gave him such ungodly counsel?

11. How did Job handle the new attack of Satan against his body and the emotional desertion of his wife?

12. What does the book of Job teach us regarding the capacity of Satan for mercy or compassion?

13. In what sense can Job be classified as an overcomer or victor in the struggles that faced him in Chapters one and two?

14. What lessons does Job teach us about the frailty of man and the folly of trusting in our strength to win spiritual battles?

15. Why do you think that Job's devotion to God caused Satan to plead for a chance to hurt him?

Chapter 4

Job's Three Friends

Now when Job's three friends heard of all this adversity that had come upon him, each one came from his own place—Eliphaz the Temanite, Bildad the Shuhite, and Zophar the Naamathite. For they had made an appointment together to come to mourn with him, and to comfort him. Job 2:11.

Job's sorrows seemed to have reached their last extreme. And now some new faces are introduced upon the scene, who are to be quite conspicuous in the remainder of the book. Three friends meet by appointment at the house of the suffering patriarch, to console him and to comfort him. The prominence accorded to them from this point onward shows that their visit is no unimportant incident, but that it is a fact of great consequence in the transaction here recorded. A very large space, and indeed the greater portion of the book, is occupied with what they say to Job, which is here reported in detail, and with what he says in reply. They are not mere spectators in a scene which deeply affects them as concerning their intimate and lifelong friend. They are themselves actors and participants, and that in a most significant and important way. They appear in the very crisis of Job's trial, in the last and most terrible stage of his sufferings, and when it would seem as though he could bear no more. They, too, are unwittingly taken into the service of the tempter, who makes use of them to add a fresh aggravation to Job's intolerable woe, which is most artfully designed to drive him to that result which Satan seeks to achieve viz., to renounce the service of the Lord.

The alternate discourses of the friends and of Job are not simply a discussion of the mysterious subject of God's afflictive providence. They are not to be removed from the circumstances in which they are uttered, which preclude an abstract treatment of a general theme. They are occupied with the case of Job, and every word uttered by his friends finds its way to the sufferer's heart. He is wounded by their harshness, stung by their accusations, exasperated by their reproaches, and driven into antagonism by their arguments. They are the professed advocates of religious obligation. They represent the cause of God, enforcing His claims on Job and justifying His ways with him, which they do in a spirit that repels him, with assumptions that experience does not sanction, and which his own inner consciousness falsifies. The unfairness, if not cruelty, with which they plead God's cause, place him under additional temptation to reject that cause itself. The hopeless variance which they assume or create between God's justice and Job's integrity, for which latter he nevertheless has the testimony of his own conscience, tends to place before his mind a distorted image of the character of God. God appears to be torturing him for crimes which he has not committed, to be relentlessly pursuing him as an implacable foe, and without justice or reason to be employing His resistless power to crush him to the earth. This is the phantom which his friends are constantly setting before him, this false notion of God as unjust and pitiless toward him; and which his own intolerable sufferings, for which he cannot himself otherwise account, seem to rivet upon him. This phantom, apparently so real, he is incessantly obliged to fight, or it would drive him to absolute despair, and force him to give up his confidence and trust in God, and thus throw him completely into the tempter's snare.

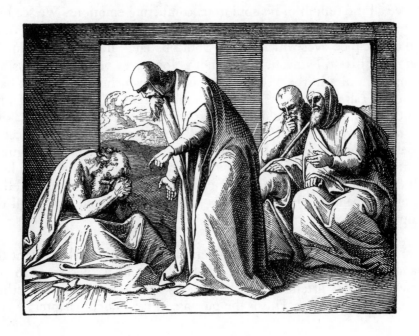

This is the point around which the conflict in Job's soul so fearfully rages, which is depicted in this book in its various phases with such a master hand. This is the very focal point of the temptation. This unwelcome argument, which his friends are constantly bringing up and dressing out before him, of a God of arbitrary power, whose justice, as they assert it, would be rank injustice, and who seems to be devoid of pity, this it is which fills him with the deepest anguish. And yet, in the darkness and the mystery of his unexplained sufferings, how is he to gain peace? To admit this conception of God, which both his own helpless misery and the arguments and assertions of his friends appear to force upon him, is to fall inevitably away from God's service. Such a God might be dreaded, but it is impossible that He could be either loved or feared.

Job's three friends, have appointed themselves as the advocates of God and the monitors of Job. They are concerned about his spiritual good, but are busily engaged in letting fly their poisoned arrows. And here is Job himself exposed without shield or buckler to their dangerous attacks. Can he sustain the weight of this new burden? Can he hold out against this fresh assault? Can his confidence in God remain unshaken when every prop is removed and the very foundations seem to be swept away? His heart is all laid open before us, down to its lowest depths, in his discourses with his friends. Everything is faithfully photographed. We see all the tumult of his soul in its conflicting emotions. We see him now sinking, now rising, now almost gone, tottering on the very verge of the precipice over which to fall would be fatal, now recoiling in the energy of his still unvanquished faith. Job gives vent to expressions wrung from him in the bitterness of his spirit, which he would not have uttered in calmer moments, until we almost dread to have him open his mouth again, lest he should in his desperation be betrayed into speaking the fatal word to which Satan by all this combination of forces is ceaselessly urging him. Job is beside himself with intolerable anguish, the terrors of God are driving him to distraction, yet through it all he is still ever and anon turning unto God and tearfully looking up to Him, his only hope and solace. Can even Job's piety still hold out? Shall the tempter at length succeed?

In order that we may the better understand how and to what extent the friends of Job aggravated his temptations, it will be necessary to pay more particular attention to the actions of these friends, and their language towards him. This is the purpose of the present chapter.

The criticism which the Lord Himself passes upon Job's friends at the close of the book, and the fact that they misapprehend as they do the cause of Job's sufferings and the purpose of God's dealings with him, has often led to an undue depreciation of their character. Against this we must carefully guard, or we shall weaken the force of the temptation so far as they are concerned, which lies greatly in this: that such men take part in it, and that they do this just as they do, and to the extent that they do.

We have reason to believe that these were eminent men, wise men, and good men. They were cherished and familiar friends of Job, such as he would naturally lean upon in a time of trouble, or turn to in perplexity for counsel and advice. They were venerable men, men of age and experience. Eliphaz says to Job: *Both the gray-haired and the aged are among us, much older than your father* (Job 15:10). We cannot think of Job, with his ten children grown up to manhood and womanhood, as at this time much less than fifty-five or sixty years old. Eliphaz in this statement probably refers to himself, since the precedence is applied to him among the friends. He in every instance speaks first, and is followed by the others, and may therefore be supposed to be their superior in age. If this be so, and he alludes to himself as "gray-haired and very aged," and "much older" than Job's father, he must have been at least as old as seventy-five or eighty. And age commanded reverence, more even then, in the patriarchal period, than with us. And it was significant of distinction, when the oldest living ancestor was the chieftain of the clan; when he was the visible lord of his descendants, and the recognized authority looked up to, deferred to, and obeyed in all their families and dependents. It was significant, too, of wisdom gathered by long experience and observation, when dealings with men and acquaintance with things rather than knowledge of books, were the chief sources of information.

The region in which Job's friends resided should also be noted, for it was proverbial for the sagacity of its inhabitants, and it is not unlikely that it is for this reason—to suggest that they were men of superior ability, of intellectual acumen, and of extensive acquirements—that the residence of each is particularly mentioned: Eliphaz the Temanite, Bildad the Shuhite and Zophar the Naamathite. Teman was famous for its wise men, and their profound sententious sayings; so was in fact Arabia, or the East, the country to which the other friends likewise belonged. To this well-known reputation of the region the prophet alludes, Jer. 49:7: *"Is wisdom no more in Teman? Has counsel perished from the prudent? Has their wisdom vanished?"* And when the wisdom of

Solomon was to be exalted by a comparison, the sacred writer says of him, I Kings 4:30: "...*Solomon's wisdom excelled the wisdom of all the men of the East....*"

And that Job's friends were worthy representatives of a land of sages is shown by their speeches here recorded, which are marked by extensive observation and careful reflection, and abound in beautiful and appropriate illustrations drawn from both nature and experience. Their reasoning is erroneous, indeed, because it is built on false premises, but their arguments are coherent and strongly put. They fail to convince or to change Job, but it is from no lack of skill in debate: they prove themselves no weak antagonists, and it requires all of Job's strength to cast off their blows. What saves him is not his superiority in argument, but that it is a matter of personal consciousness about which they contend. No subtleties and no cogency of demonstration can convict him of offenses of which his own conscience pronounces him innocent. They misinterpret the ways of providence, and fail to explain the mystery of Job's sufferings. But this is from no mental incapacity. Job can see no farther into this dark mystery than they can. He knows that they are mistaken. But he no more understands the real state of the case than they do. The fact is that the enigma is insoluble by the unaided reason of man. God alone can declare the purpose of His afflictive actions, and this He had never yet revealed. These distresses of Job were to afford the occasion of shedding the first rays of light upon it. It is no discredit to the friends any more than to Job that they did not discern what they had no means of knowing. In what they really were to blame, and to what extent, we shall soon consider.

They were, moreover, good men, and had a heart of real affection for Job. The whole tenor of their speeches shows that they were concerned both for the honor of God and for the spiritual welfare of Job. They advocate and approve what is good; they reject and condemn the bad. Their discourses sparkle with gems of morality and religious truth. The principles which they propound are mostly just as general truths. It is only the application which they make of them to a case that they do not really understand, which is false. They entertain a true friendship for Job; but their assessment of him and his trials warps their judgment; and, in their desire to reclaim him from imaginary wrong doing, they are themselves guilty of actual though unintended injustice, and treat him with undo severity.

The friends of Job, then, as we may conceive, were men of distinction, eminent for wisdom and of approved piety, worthy confidants and intimates of Job, trusted and tried doubtless in the companionship of years. They hear of the great sorrows of their friend, and they show their attachment to him by agreeing to meet at his house to mourn with him and to comfort him. They bring him in actual fact but little comfort, it is true; but this is the design and expectation with which they come. It is important to observe the change which takes place in the friends regarding their feelings and attitude towards Job in the progress of the book. This is depicted with admirable art, and is essential to a proper understanding of the whole story. To impute to them from the beginning of their visit the harsh and ungenerous attitude which they come to express later in their visit, is to mistake their character entirely, and to lose sight of that inward change in their sentiments respecting Job which is so skillfully drawn and is so true to nature. The longer the friends argue with Job without convincing him, the more stubborn and incorrigible he appears to them, and the more severe is the judgment which they are disposed to pass upon him.

They come with sympathy and sorrow for him in his griefs. Finding him so changed that they no longer recognize him, they are brought to tears. *"They lifted their voices and wept; and each one tore his robe and sprinkled dust on his head toward heaven. So they sat down with him on the ground seven days and seven nights, and no one spoke a word to him, for they saw that his grief was very great"* (Job 2:12, 13). They could not more tenderly and delicately express their commiseration for him in his terrible sorrow, which it was beyond the power of human helpers to relieve. In all this there was genuine pity and compassion. There is no room for supposing that they entertained any other than the most friendly feelings, or that any ungenerous suspicions had as yet taken possession of their minds as to the reality of Job's piety or the reasons for these extraordinary sufferings which had been sent upon him.

Job first breaks the mournful silence by his outburst of lamentation, brought on by unbearable distress. Eliphaz, probably the eldest and most respected of the three friends, as he is certainly the most dignified and courteous in his style of address, first makes reply. And, as Job answers him, he is successively followed by Bildad and by Zophar. As the interview still proceeds, and Job continues to respond, the friends once more address themselves to him in the same order; and yet again the third time. Only in the third and last series of discourses the third friend, Zophar, fails to speak, for a reason to be stated hereafter. Eliphaz and Bildad accordingly each speak three times, and Zophar twice, Job invariably responding. There is thus a triple series of discourses, in which the growing alienation and distrust of the friends can be plainly traced. They begin with comparative mildness and expressions of regard. But, as the discussion advances, they are astounded and excited by Job's opposition to what they consider primary principles of religious faith. They are provoked and incensed by his stubborness, his lack of submission to the divine will, and by his attitude, which appears to them to savor of irreverence. By the end of their discussions, they lose all confidence in his uprightness and sincerity, and believe him to have been secretly guilty of the most atrocious and outrageous crimes.

When Job, begins to utter his frantic grief, and curses the day in which he was born, Eliphaz feels called upon to verbally correct Job. He makes an endeavor in this first speech to rouse his friend from his utter despondency, to remind him of the moral reasons for this terrible infliction, and to exhort him to that more complete submission which would be followed by the return of God's favor, and by more than his former prosperity.

He begins in an apologetic and insinuating strain: *"If one attempts a word with you, Will you become weary? But who can withhold himself from speaking?"* (Job 4:2) He then proceeds by bidding Job remember how he had strengthened and comforted others in their affliction; and he ought not now to show weakness himself. As a good and righteous man, he should not despond, but hope in God, who would not suffer the innocent to perish, nor the righteous to be cut off. As to the source of his troubles, he reminds him of the universal sinfulness of men. Mortal man cannot be just in the sight of God, nor man pure before his Maker. Men are sinners; hence their frail and perishable nature. They are crushed before the moth, they are destroyed from morning to evening. Affliction cometh not forth from the dust, neither doth trouble spring out of the ground. They arise from no extraneous sources. But man is born to trouble as the sparks fly upward. He is involved in it by a necessity of his nature: it springs directly out of his inborn sinfulness. Hence he admonishes him to submit his case humbly and trustfully to God, under whose universal and righteous providence the poor hath hope, and iniquity is compelled to stop her mouth. *"He shall deliver you in six troubles, Yes, in seven no evil shall touch you"* (Job 5:19). And he concludes by describing in beautiful and impressive terms the happy consequences of submissively accepting the Lord's correction.

To this rational and elegant speech of Eliphaz, there are two exceptions to be taken. In the first place, it could not but grate harshly on the ears of Job that his friend should expect him to endure his lengthy and bitter sufferings with perfect calmness. As though there were no limits to human endurance, and it were possible to bear up under misery like his without a word of complaint. The sobs and groans and lamentations wrung from him by an anguish too severe to be quietly endured is surely a weakness that is not to be too harshly judged. And the appeal to Job's piety, as though this should have quieted his clamor and led him still to maintain a cheerful hope amidst his overwhelming distress, showed a lack of consideration for the condition in which he then was. There was in all this a lack of that tenderness and that appreciative sympathy which was a prime requisite in one who would comfort such a mourner as Job.

The second point open to criticism in the discourse of Eliphaz in not a matter of feeling, like the preceding, but of principle. It is the manner in which he represents sin and suffering as linked together in God's providential dealings, as though this afforded an adequate explanation of every case of affliction, Job's included. This point is so skillfully put, that what he actually says can scarcely be objected to: it is only what he implies, by offering this as the solution of the case in hand. He brings no harsh or doubtful charge against Job. He expresses no suspicion, and apparently entertains none. His plea is rather based on the assumption that Job is really what he has ever been supposed to be in uprightness and the devout fear of God.

He lays no accusation upon him but such as is common to all who are sharers of our degenerate nature. All are impure in the sight of God, and all are in consequence born to trouble. Exposure to suffering, and suffering itself, is an inevitable result of that corrupt nature with which we were born. The wise and reasonable course, and the truly godly response, is not to indulge in passionate outcries against the divine orderings, which can only produce harm to the sufferer himself (v.2). Rather, it is wise to meekly accept and submit to the sorrows which He sends, who makes sore and binds up, who wounds and His hands make whole. Such submission will surely lead to peace and to salvation.

It is undoubtedly true that where there is no sin there will be no suffering among the subjects of God's moral government. All suffering has sin as its invariable and necessary antecedent. It is also true that the consciousness of sin must forever close the mouth of every sufferer from any well-grounded complaint against the righteousness of God. The holiest and the best are sinners nevertheless. And whatever may be the sufferings they endure in the providence of God, it cannot be said that they are unjustly treated. For, as Zophar states in more developed form to Job, "... *God exacts from you Less than your iniquity deserves*" (Job 11:6). No man's sufferings in this world are equal to what he deserves.

But, while this is true and incontestable, it does not account for cases of special and extraordinary suffering, and especially such as occur in the experience of good men, such as we have here in Job's case. The general sinfulness of men may account for human sorrows so far as they are uniformly distributed. And a like principle may be applied where they are plainly visible in proportion to the demerit of the sufferers. But special suffering, not involving special guilt, cannot be accounted for in this way. A sinfulness common to all cannot be the reason why one is singled out rather than another, and made to endure extraordinary sorrows.

The special significance of suffering, therefore, remains unexplained. Its importance as a means of discipline and training, and the far more exceeding reward by which it shall be abundantly compensated, are not once suspected. Eliphaz alleges that man suffers because he is a sinner. He did not know that a man may likewise suffer because he is a saint, that he may thus exhibit more distinctly his godly character, that he may be ripened still more in holiness, and that his final reward may be proportionately increased. To Eliphaz, suffering was ever and only a punishment, a judgment for sin, an infliction of the divine displeasure. He did not know that it might also be a token of love, a means of grace, a blessing in disguise; that whom the Lord loves He chastens, scourging every son He receives.

The other friends, in their discourses, follow Eliphaz in the principles and method of discussion, only with increased vehemence and more open criticism of Job. Their focus is that God cannot deal unjustly, and therefore suffering must be the fruit of sin. Bildad intimates that Job's children had but suffered the consequences of their own misdeeds, so that this loss which he had experienced was the result of sin, not his own indeed, but theirs. And he puts an 'if' before his affirmation of the piety of Job himself, "*If you were pure and upright, Surely now He would awake for you, And prosper your rightful habitation.*" (Job 8:6). Zophar puts the 'if' before the contrary hypothesis as to Job's character and conduct, implying at least the possibility, "*If iniquity were in your hand, and you put it far away, And would not let wickedness dwell in your tents; Then surely you could lift up your face without spot; Yes, you could be steadfast, and not fear; Because you would forget your misery, And remember it as waters that have passed away, And your life would be*

48

brighter than noonday. Though you were dark, you would be like the morning." (Job 11:14-17) The vividness and beauty of the imagery which they employ, and the force and vigor of their expressions, cannot fail to charm and to impress, however unsatisfactory their treatment of the mystery with which they deal, however unsound or rather one-sided the conclusions to which they come—and however unjust and ungenerous they may be in accusing Job.

When Eliphaz speaks a second time, it is plain that he has undergone a considerable change in his feelings toward Job. He reasserts the fundamental principle in common with the other friends, of the necessary connection of suffering with sin. But he no longer illustrates or defends it by the consideration of the universal sinfulness of humanity. It is not of man as *"born to trouble"* that he now speaks, so much as of man *"who drinks iniquity like water."* It is the fate of the ungodly and wicked man that he holds up before Job for his warning. And instead of presupposing Job's integrity, and urging him in consequence to cherish the hope that he should not be utterly cut off, he charges him rather with serious guilt. It is true that he does not charge Job with criminal misdeeds or acts of sin, but with wicked words. In his speeches now uttered in the presence of the friends he has fallen from grace. He has maintained principles and uttered expressions inconsistent with pious reverence for God. *"You do away with fear, and take away prayer before God."* That is to say, Job, you are putting an end to holiness and are emptying prayer of its value by the sentiments which you have voiced here. *"For your iniquity teaches your mouth, And you choose the tongue of the crafty. Your own mouth condemns you, and not I; Yes, your own lips testify against you"* (Job 15:5-6).

Bildad and Zophar once more follow Eliphaz in the same general strain, holding up before Job the destruction that is certain, sooner or later, to overtake the ungodly. And they intimate plainly that this is the explanation of the dismal things which have befallen him.

Eliphaz in his third discourse makes a further advance. He now, without any ambiguity of language or indirectness explicitly charges Job with the most atrocious wickedness. He has become more and more distant from him as the discussion has proceeded. He has become more and more convinced from the language of Job himself that he is destitute of real holiness. In truth, all his former confidence in Job has utterly vanished, and he not only believes him capable of any amount of wickedness, but he is persuaded that he has actually perpetrated crimes of the most serious character. Eliphaz believes that the sorrows by which

Job has so suddenly and so fearfully been overwhelmed are thus easily accounted for.

It is not now the general sinfulness of human nature which he lays before him, as in his first discourse. Nor does he merely allege the language of irreverence to be found in his speeches which he had here uttered in their presence, as in his second discourse. Nor does he content himself with indirect insinuations that his fate was but the customary fate of the wicked, as the other friends had already done. But he goes beyond all this and makes open and direct charges of habitual and gross transgression. *"Is not your wickedness great, And your iniquity without end? For you have taken pledges from your brother for no reason, And stripped the naked of their clothing. You have not given the weary water to drink, And you have withheld bread from the hungry.... You have sent widows away empty, And the strength of the fatherless was crushed. Therefore snares are all around you, And sudden fear troubles you"* (Job 22:5-10). A just and all-seeing God has detected the villainy and set the brand of His judgment upon it. Eliphaz thinks that Job is suffering just what might be expected as the righteous reward for the iniquity which he had practiced. Job's imagined security was at an end, and deserved vengeance has overtaken him at last.

What a spectacle this is! And what a lesson we may learn here. This man is one whom God has declared to be without equal for holiness, a perfect and upright man, one who feared God and turned away from evil. And yet here are good and wise men, men of age and experience, his friends through many former years, knowing him not merely by reputation but by personal acquaintance, who do not hesitate to cherish the grossest and most unjust suspicions, and actually to charge him with the most vicious type of misconduct. And they do all this without the slightest foundation in actual fact! It is purely their wild speculations which underlie their charges. Yet they lay it upon him as though they had the most undoubted evidence of its reality. Again we say, what a spectacle! What a lesson we may learn here!

These friends of Job, we have admitted, are not to blame for not knowing what could only be known by divine revelation—and we know what had not then been revealed. It does not imply any moral blindness nor any dullness of intellectual perception that they could not discern the true intent of the sufferings of Job, or the divine purpose in permitting them. This was a secret still undisclosed. The mystery of the afflictions of the righteous was now to be unveiled as it had never been before. And the sufferings of Job were to furnish the occasion for the lessons which God was to teach. But this was not to be done until gifted minds, well instructed in the general truths of religion at the time, had grappled with the problem and had shown by the trial the incompetency of unaided reason to solve the riddle. The ignorance of Job's friends, and of Job himself, regarding the meaning and design of God's dealings with him, was not reprehensible. This could not have been otherwise, for they could not know.

In regard to ignorance then they are excusable. But what cannot be excused in them is that in the first place they undertook to expound what they did not understand, acting as though they had full knowledge in the case. In so doing, they assessed the purposes of God in light of human reason, seeking to explain it by their own limited notions. If they had confessed the mystery and admitted their ignorance, all would have been well. They would have saved themselves from the errors and mistakes, the gross injustices which they visited upon Job. By acting as they did, they in fact dishonored the providence of God, which they were professedly defending. They prescribed a rule for its administration as the only one compatible with justice, which is not, after all, the method which it actually follows. Suffering is not distributed according to the ratio nor on the principles which they allege to be absolutely demanded by God's essential attributes. By defending God's actions on grounds which are wholly inadequate, they do their utmost, though unwittingly, to bring them into discredit.

And in the second place, they were inexcusable in another respect. They not only entered a weak and unsuitable plea as the only one upon which the cause of God could be rested or His providence justified, but they likewise undertook to bolster up His cause by a phony, if not positively immoral method. As Job charges upon them (Job 13:7), they spoke wickedly for God, they talked deceitfully for Him. They accused Job of things which they, by experience or evidence, had no means of knowing to be true—and which, in fact, were not true. They inferred from false premises, and were willing to conduct the defense of the divine government in this way. They were guilty of making rash and reckless assertions as they professed to defend the cause of true religion. They were unjust to Job, not only harboring baseless suspicions, but in venturing upon positive declarations of his guilt in matters of which he was wholly innocent. They were shamefully cruel to their suffering friend, a friend which supposedly they had come to soothe. Job's friends should have been able to see that he was already weighed down by troubles that should have disarmed malice itself and softened hearts of stone. Nothing in their argument could justify a strategy like this. If

God's righteous government could not be honestly and truthfully defended without resorting to what is questionable and false, they should have concluded that they were not called of God to be His champions in this situation. They should have admitted the mystery and confessed their ignorance, and waited patiently till the Lord Himself disclosed the basis on which He chose to have His cause rested. Confiding in Him who does great, unsearchable things, and whose ways are past finding out, they should have trusted that he would make all plain in His own good time. Instead, they presume to put forth unholy hands to support the ark of God, and darkened His infinite counsel by words without knowledge.

The gross charges put forth by Eliphaz could not be repeated by Bildad in his speech, which followed, in the face of Job's solemn insistence of his innocence, and his appeal to the omniscient Judge of all. Accordingly he recedes from them entirely, falling back on the original position of Eliphaz in his opening speech; viz., the universal sinfulness of men, in which Job is of necessity involved. He thus by implication not only retracts the charges previously made against Job, but concedes his inability to conduct the argument further. He has nothing to add but what had been said and answered long before. The same thing is likewise intimated by the brevity of his speech, which consists of but a few commonplace sentences. And Zophar makes no attempt to speak at all!

The friends decide to give up their argument with Job. They cannot convince or convict him. They entered their protest against his complaint in his wild outburst of grief. They sought to convict him of the irreverence and impiety of which they thought him guilty, and to bring him back to what they esteemed right views and a proper spirit. Instead of this they threw themselves upon the side of the great adversary. They became the tools and accomplices of Satan in his sore temptation, giving all their weight to the side opposed to God and goodness, while embittering Job against a cause which was upheld by such methods. They tempted Job to renounce the service of God Himself, whom they represented in a light that served only to repel.

The question has now reached its utmost intensity. Can Job withstand the temptation which is brought to bear upon him with all this accumulated force? With his property swept away, his children gone, himself the victim of a loathsome and painful disease, his own wife begging him to abandon the service of a God so cruel as to be the author of all their woes, his agony, both of body and of mind, still growing, without the prospect of release—and now the trusted friends of former years deserting and scorning him, stinging him with their undeserved reproaches, while he himself is totally unable to comprehend the righteousness or the reasons behind these dreadful inflictions—can Job bear it all, still maintaining his unswerving trust in God. The answer is to be found in Job's successive replies to his friends, in which all the workings of his soul in this fearful crisis are so vividly and faithfully portrayed. The examination of these replies are now before us. May He, who alone can, uphold and comfort all His tried and suffering saints help us to understand Job.

CHAPTER 4: COMPREHENSION QUESTIONS

Job's Three Friends

1. What were the names of the three men who came to visit Job after his second battle with Satan?

2. Do you think that Job's friends were foolish to give Job a good deal of "quiet time" before they spoke?

3. Why do Christians need to be careful when they are purporting to represent the views of Almighty God?

4. Did the author believe that it was fair to characterize Job's three friends as foolish and uncaring men?

5. In what respect do Job's friends teach us that we cannot always judge a situation by outward circumstances?

6. Describe the downward progress of Job's friends as they moved deeper into a heated debate with him?

7. How many times do Eliphaz, Bildad, and Zophar speak during Job's trial?

8. What did Eliphaz say regarding the supposed link between sin and suffering? Do you agree with his position?

9. Although Job often conceded the general truthfulness of the points made by his friends, he still disagreed with their attempts to apply those truths to his personal situation. Was Job just

being stubborn in his refusal to acknowledge the points made by his friends?

10. How do you think Job's perspective on the reliability of human friendships was affected by the way his three friends treated him?

11. What are some of the dangers that stem from trying to argue with someone without full knowledge of the facts?

12. Why do you think that it is so hard for people to admit that they do not understand a particular situation or event?

13. Did Job's three friends end up convincing Job that he was guilty of following an immoral path in his life?

14. What was the true source of strength that enabled Job to cling to God even though all of his physical senses and emotions left him without hope?

15. Do you think that the peace that God gives to each of his spiritual children is capable of being understood on strictly worldly terms? Please explain your answer.

Chapter 5

Job's Conflict

My friends scorn me, My eyes pour out tears to God. Job 16: 20.

Satan now has his plan completely laid, and it would almost seem as though he ultimately has his victim entirely in his power, and there was no escape out of the fatal snare. Job, with all he had, was put at the disposal of the evil one, with the single limitation that he must spare his life. And Satan has used the liberty accorded to him aggressively. He has brought the most frightful complication of sorrows and sufferings upon the unsuspecting patriarch, and set every influence at work that he could bring to bear upon him, to overturn his integrity and detach Him from the service of God. Can he succeed in his fiendish purpose?

He has crushed the spirit of Job and quenched his hopes. He has heaped pain and grief upon him, until, in the depth of his anguish, existence itself has become an insupportable burden. The weary sufferer, stunned, bewildered, tortured to the last extreme of despair, curses the day that he was born, and longs for nothing so much as to die. It would seem as though Job could hold out no longer. Satan perceives his advantage in this crisis of Job's misery, and presses it relentlessly, through the use of his friends, who unwittingly align themselves on the tempter's side. These professed ministers of consolation and advocates of piety treat him in a manner which embitters him against them and the cause which they defend. Their pleas for the equity of the divine administration are repugnant to his sense of right, and to the testimony of his own conscience. They represent his aggravated sufferings as a righteous retribution, either for the sinfulness inborn in our common human nature, or for the sin revealed in his present unsubmissive speeches, or for the guilt of some gross criminality now first detected and brought to light. These assumptions Job repels point by point. His sufferings cannot be so explained. What, then, is the inevitable alternative? Is not God unrighteous? Or is He not at least like an implacable foe, mercilessly inflicting upon him these grievous sorrows? If woe like this be not the reward of justice, must it not be injustice or wanton cruelty? And, if God be either unjust or pitiless, how can the sufferer, crushed beneath His arbitrary inflictions, adore or trust Him?

Job's triumph is, in the most absolute and unqualified sense, the triumph of faith over human reason or logic. He seems to outward view to have no ground left to stand upon. Satan has apparently forced him to conclusions respecting the providence of God, which positively exclude worship. It would seem as though everything conspired to show that God was persecuting him, and treating him as an enemy. Yet from an angry God he can turn nowhere but back to God Himself, in whom he does and must confide, in spite of his apparent hostility. God is still his only refuge, even from the fierceness of His own displeasure. *"Though He slay me, yet will I trust Him"* (Job 13:15).

Job's triumph was not easily gained. He was pressed and abused by Satan to the fullest extent. The struggle was desperate, and tested his faithfulness to the utmost. The contest was not simply one of fortitude and human courage to bear up under calamities and sufferings, and to rise superior to that terrible combination of distresses which was weighing him down. The question to be settled was not whether Job had that heroic firmness and indomitable self-control, or rather self-sufficiency, and could calmly bear all outward losses, and support undisturbed the most grievous pain and sorrow. His trial lay in a totally different plane. The point of it was, whether he would still cleave to God and maintain his trust in Him, when there no longer remained anything external to attract him to His service. Everything combined to repel him and drive him from his Maker. In essence the main point illustrated the fact that the substance of faith cannot be seen or analyzed by human reason. Faith is the substance of things unseen and is given and upheld by God Himself.

The hand of God was in these dreadful sorrows. Why had He sent them, or permitted them? The Christian can readily answer this question, and can comprehend with less difficulty how afflictions are consistent with the divine goodness and love. But the revelations which shed such a cheerful light for us upon this mysterious subject had not then been given. Job was left to confront the difficulty with no help afforded him for its solution. He was in utter darkness and perplexity and unable to apprehend the reasons for his trial. And the only solution which offered itself, and towards which he was persistently driven by antagonism, was not reconcilable with the goodness or justice of God. Reason and sense urge him in one direction, and the strong recoil of faith drives him back in the other; and thus he is swayed perpetually to and fro, still hoping against hope, ever afresh seeking unto God who is silent. Job was unable to escape from conclusions to which the logic of his sufferings seemed to constrain him, or to banish the forbidding specter of an angry God which they perpetually raised before him. Yet, he held fast to his inmost convictions, in spite of all that seemed to contradict them.

This inward struggle of Job is not made the subject of any formal description, but it is vividly depicted in his successive speeches in reply to his friends. These lay bare all the workings of his soul, and the fearful agitation which was going on within him. They disclose the terrible conflict through which he was passing, in its various phases, until out of the depths of despair he found the peace that passes all understanding. They show into what distress the tempter plunged him; what gloom and darkness had settled upon his path; to what spiritual straits he was reduced; but how in spite of all he never abandoned his faith in God. He staggered and tottered under the tremendous blows which were given him, and it seemed at times as though he could not recover himself, and must fall. But somehow, through the unseen grace of God he always regained his footing, and never lost his balance entirely. The adversary was foiled, notwithstanding all the weapons he employed. And the faith of Job, which he sought to undermine or to destroy, sustained the test and triumphed in the encounter.

Job's opening speech, in which he first breaks silence and pours forth his piteous expression of woe, is a soliloquy. It is the melancholy wail of insupportable anguish. It is the frantic outburst of grief, which has been held in until it can no longer be repressed, and to which he now gives vent, apparently unconscious that others are present, bemoaning himself without the thought of being overheard. The burden of his speech is the misery of this intolerable existence: "Oh that I had never lived! Oh that now I might cease to be!"

When Eliphaz and the other friends undertake to address him, Job directs his replies partly to them and partly to God. He speaks to his friends with the double aim of exciting their pity and replying to their arguments. What he says to God is likewise of a twofold character: he both wrestles with God, in the way of complaint for the misery which God has inflicted upon him, and he affirms his confidence in Him. It is in these addresses to God that his inward agony most fully asserts itself. The mixed emotions with which his soul is torn asunder meet in the sharpest contrast and collision, and he undergoes the greatest and most sudden transitions of feeling.

The progress and the stages of Job's inward strife are very plainly marked. His ineffectual appeals to his friends for the sympathy which they deny him throw him back more and more upon God as his only source of help. Refused the pity that he craves on earth, he can look nowhere but to Heaven, and is forced to seek his only refuge there. Accordingly, that which overwhelmingly occupies his mind in the first instance is the relation between himself and God. Is God his Enemy, or is He his Friend? Despair and hope struggle for the mastery, and the conflict grows more and more intense until the climax is reached at the central point of the discussion between him and his friends. Corresponding to the three series of speeches addressed to Job by his three friends, who follow each other in the same invariable order, are the three series of his replies severally addressed to them. Throughout the first series of Job's responses, and into the middle of the second the conflict in his soul continues to heighten, until in his second reply to his second friend, Bildad, it attains its height. Here the conflicting opinions come to their most intense encounter. His sense of the hostility of God to him reaches its most vivid and vehement expression, but is immediately succeeded and swallowed up by the conviction which overspreads his soul of the certainty of God's friendship and favor, which, though the worst comes to the worst, must and will manifest itself. This deliverance will come now, or in the world to come. With this burst of triumph the temptation loses its strength. Satan is vanquished, and Job's inward conflict is substantially over. Faith has secured the victory. He has gained the assurance that God is his Redeemer, come what may and in spite of all adverse appearances. And with this the whole power of the temptation is broken.

The darkness is not quickly dispersed. The mystery of the works of God is no nearer its solution. The seeming contradictions remain, and are as unexplainable as ever. Why he has been made to suffer or allowed to suffer so terribly he does not know. He has not the faintest idea of the reasons for the infliction. He does not discern how it is to be reconciled with the goodness of God, or His righteousness, or His favor towards himself. But he has laid hold of hope with the strong grasp of faith. He is assured that God is his Redeemer and his Friend; and his confident trust does not again give way. Notwithstanding the continuance of his sufferings and the difficulties that darken their explanation, he is now on the solid rock. The floods may dash around him, but they cannot break over him; and he is no longer in peril of being overwhelmed. His faith is revealing itself in hope strengthened.

Having thus reached comparative peace, and settled the question which chiefly agitated him regarding his relationship to God, Job next turns his attention more immediately to his controversy with his friends. He has rejected the points of their position before, and stated facts at variance with it; but in his subsequent speeches, viz.. the last of the second series and in those of the third series, he refutes their position by reviewing their arguments in detail, and he shows that they have furnished no adequate or satisfactory account of God's providence in general or of his sorrows in particular.

Having thus hastily sketched in outline the flow of Job's feelings toward God and his attitude toward his friends, we may now return to take a more deliberate survey of his various speeches, with the view of noting more minutely his demeanor at each successive step of his great struggle.

In his first reply to Eliphaz, Job is in the same state of unrelieved despair as in his opening complaint. The sympathy of his friends had been denied him, and he bitterly scolds them for withholding that pity which was so needful to him in his distressed situation, and would have cost them so little. Eliphaz had reminded him of the infinite greatness of God, and of the feebleness and frailty of sinful man, and urged these as reasons why he should be submissive under his sufferings. To Job's mind these are but an aggravation of his misery and a fresh justification of his complaint. He had but one brief life to live, and this was filled up with weariness and woe, *"Therefore,"* he says, *"I will not restrain my mouth; I will speak in the anguish of my spirit; I will complain in the bitterness of my soul"* (Job 7:11). And he converts these into pleas with the Almighty that he would mitigate the severity of his treatment. He was too insignificant and frail, sinner though he was, to deserve or to require such terrible testing from the infinite God.

There does not appear to be a single ray of comfort nor a gleam of hope for the stricken sufferer in the present or the future, from man or from God. But from this abyss of darkness and cheerless despondency he struggles constantly upward towards the light. In each successive speech some slight advance is made; there is each time some fresh reaching out towards help or hope. Every address made by his friends shows him more and more plainly that nothing is to be looked for or expected from them: they still persist in refusing to him even that measure of relief or consolation which human sympathy might supply. Cut off from all earthly assistance or even pity, there is no one but God to whom he can have recourse. And here he is torn by conflicting feelings. God is persecuting and afflicting him, and, to all outward appearance, is treating him as an enemy. And still he cannot let go that inward persuasion, which manifests itself at first dimly, and yet grows in clearness and strength as he holds to it, that God will not altogether withhold his favor from him. Each time that he attempts to speak, sense and faith stand in blank antagonism. His sufferings press overwhelmingly upon him with their apparent evidence that God is against him. But Faith comes with its whispers, scarcely audible, and yet refusing to be stifled, that God must nevertheless be on his side. The spiritual realm becomes increasing real to Job as he senses the Lord's presence uplifting his inner man.

These suggestions of his unquenched confidence in God are only hypothetical at first. If such an obstacle were only removed, or if such a condition could only exist, then God would surely manifest Himself in his favor. But the obstacle remains; the condition is impossible to be realized; and so he sinks back each time into a state of unrelieved depression. But his despair is no longer absolute and total. These principles of faith and hope gradually assume a more definite form, and take upon themselves more reality. They gain in strength, and come to a fuller expression with each successive response he makes to his friends, until at last they grow into a clear and decided conviction which removes the clouds of despondency. Faith breaks through the trap which the adversary has thrown around him, and vanquishes the power of the temptation by the language of triumphant assurance, "I know that my Redeemer liveth."

In the reply to Bildad, the second of the friends, we see the first budding of this rising hope, the first glimmer of the coming dawn. We witness the earliest suggestion of a more favorable issue; but it is a suggestion clogged with an impossible condition, and which cannot be realized in the form in which it presents itself to his mind. If he could but speak with God on equal terms, if God would lay aside His infinite majesty and divest Himself of His awful terrors, then he would present his case before Him and it would be acceptably heard, and he would be vindicated by his Judge. But how is such a hearing to be obtained? "... *He is not a man, as I am, That I may answer him, And that we should go to court together. Nor is there any mediator between us, Who may lay his hand on us both*" (Job 9:32, 33). He, nevertheless, pleads with God for His righteousness' sake and for His past mercies, upon which he fondly dwells, not to destroy him. *"I will say to God, 'Do not condemn me; Show me why You contend with me. Does it seem good to You that You should oppress, That You should despise the work of Your hands, And shine on the counsel of the wicked' "* (Job 10:2-3).

When Zophar, the last of the friends, speaks, it is in the same strain with those who had preceded him, only with greater harshness. If Job had hung onto an expectation of pity or even justice from at least one of his friends, this is now gone. And he responds in terms of bitter and indignant rebuke for their arrogant conceit in emphasizing the familiar aspects of God's justice, as though they were an adequate solution of the mysteries of His providence. These rest on totally different and as yet unexplained grounds. They were undertaking to defend God's providence in a manner which would not be sanctioned by God Himself. He was confident, therefore, that God would declare in his favor and not in theirs. He was sure of a vindication, if his case could only come before God. And his mind returns again to the same twofold obstruction as before; and the likelihood of its removal, though doubtful and distant, does not seem so absolutely impossible as before. *"Only two things do not to me,… Withdraw Your hand far from me, And let not the dread of You make me afraid. Then call, and I will answer; Or let me speak, then You respond to me"* (Job 13:20-22).

But the sense of his misery returns upon him, and of his life almost at an end, cut off amidst his hopeless sufferings; and what possibility remains of a divine restoration?

"For there is hope for a tree, If it is cut down, that it will sprout again, And that its tender shoots will not cease. But man dies and is laid away; Indeed he breathes his last, And where is he? As water disappears from the sea, And a river becomes parched and dries up, So man lies down and does not rise. Till the heavens are no more, They will not awake, Nor be roused from their sleep" (Job 14:7, 10-12). Oh if it were otherwise! If death were but a temporary suspension of his earthly life! If he could go down to the grave for a season, until God's favor were restored to him, and then could return to the land of the living and come back to his former abode, he would patiently endure all that was laid upon him now. *"Oh, that You would hide me in the grave, That You would conceal me until Your wrath is past, That You would appoint me a set time, and remember me! If a man dies, shall he live again? All the days of my hard service I will wait, Till my change comes"* (Job 14:13-14) my restoration from death to life.

Job is trembling here on the verge of a hope full of immortality, which is soon to assume its proper form before his mind and to swell to its just dimensions. But it is as yet only inadequately conceived by him. A conscious state of existence beyond the grave was part of the faith of the early patriarchs, who looked forward to being "gathered to their fathers." But the future state was then revealed only in the most dim and shadowy outline. It was to them an unseen and unknown world; no bright and joyous anticipations were connected with it, no clear disclosures had yet been made regarding it. The bare fact of its reality was almost all that was known. The veil was about to be lifted to the wrestling soul of Job, further than it had ever been raised to human eyes before. The lesson of his immortality was one of special value for his present need. And he is here darkly and vaguely feeling after it, and reaching out towards it. In all his previous speeches, the grave has been the end of all that he expected or hoped for—not, we may assume, the end of being and conscious spiritual existence, but of life in any desirable sense. He had no anticipations of good in the grave or beyond it, no thought of blessedness in another state, which could outweigh or alleviate his present sorrows. All his notions of the future were negative. He conceived of it simply as a state empty of all earthly good. He had no idea of the positive blessings belonging to it, of its bliss and glory with God. He looked downward to Sheol, the land of ghosts and shades, not upward to heaven, the abode of glorified spirits in the immediate presence of God Himself.

The mists that shrouded the future would never be substantially taken away until Jesus Christ abolished death, and brought life and immortality to light through the gospel. The apostles and disciples of Christ stand in an entirely different attitude to the future world, and hold a different language respecting it from the saints of God, who preceded his coming. The consciousness that to die is gain, the desire to depart as far better than to abide in the flesh, belongs wholly to the New Testament: it has no parallel in the Old. Nevertheless, preliminary lessons of great value were already given during Old Testament times. One of the first gleams of heavenly light sent to lighten the darkness of the grave is found in the book of Job. It is born of an assurance graciously imputed to Job's soul as he struggled with his terrible temptation.

In all that he had said previously of death, it has been spoken of as terminating every hope and every joyful prospect. *"As the cloud disappears and vanishes away, So he who goes down to the grave does not come up. He shall never return to his house, Nor shall his place know him anymore"* (Job 7:9, 10). *"Before I go to the place from which I shall not return, To the land of darkness and the shadow of death, A land as dark as darkness itself, As the shadow of death, without any order, Where even the light is like darkness"* (Job 10: 21, 22). But in the speech to Zophar upon which we are now remarking, he ventures the hypothetical suggestion of a return again to life from the dead. If that were only possible, it would relieve the gloom of this dark situation under which he is suffering. It would allay the strife, which now rages in his soul between his conviction that God will declare on his behalf, and the outward appearance as though God were his foe. It would open the way to a reconciliation between these seeming contradictions. It would afford an opportunity for the divine favor, of which he was inwardly assured, still to manifest itself to him. In the precise form in which this vague suggestion has arisen in his mind, it cannot again be renewed. And with this impossibility he relapses into his former state of cheerless despondency. But the germ of hope is there, which will soon unfold itself in a more practicable form to the assured conviction of God's favor manifested to him in a future life.

The temptation is now approaching its crisis, and Job's inward conflict is becoming more and more intense. In his next two speeches he says little, almost nothing, to his friends. He merely in a few words at the beginning gives vent to his impatience at their unfeeling speeches, and begs them to desist and torture him no longer. He makes no reply to their arguments, but turns from them to God and pours forth all the agitation of his soul before Him. Despair and hope are in his bosom, and the struggle is a fearful one indeed. His agony and inward distress are at their highest point, and are reflected in the vehemence and even passionate character of his expressions. He is bowed down by the sense of God's anger as apparently shown in these terrible inflictions. *"He tears me in His wrath, and hates me; He gnashes at me with His teeth; ... I was at ease, but He has shattered me; He also has taken me by my neck, and shaken me to pieces; He has set me up for His target, His archers surround me. He pierces my heart and does not pity; He pours out my gall on the ground. He breaks me with wound upon wound; He runs at me like a warrior. My face is flushed from weeping, And on my eyelids is the shadow of death;..."* (Job 16:9, 12-14, 16).

And all this, as his inward consciousness of integrity and his total inability to comprehend why God should have treated him thus, prompt him to exclaim, "Not for any injustice in mine hands: also my prayer is pure." Such violent treatment, which he has no consciousness of having deserved, dealing with him as though he were a gross

63

offender, which he was not, and carrying the infliction even to the point of destroying his life, extorts from him the passionate outcry as from the victim of atrocious injury: "O earth, do not cover my blood, And let my cry have no resting place" (Job 16:18). I must die, but it is unrighteous murder. Let the earth refuse to drink in my blood thus unjustly shed, so that it may remain forever exposed, a constant witness to the terrible wrong perpetrated upon me; and let my death-cry never be hushed to silence, but resound forever in testimony of the cruel violence under which I suffer. I die, unable longer to sustain these dreadful inflictions which God is bringing upon me; but I die, protesting against the injustice and the outrage.

Has Satan then gained his end, and has Job at length fallen into the snare? In the frightful darkness, which has to outward view obscured the evidence of God's integrity, has Job given up his sense of honoring God? Is his confidence in God's eternal justice gone? Then has he indeed been driven to that renunciation of God's service to which Satan has relentlessly endeavored to force him?

But no! In all this agony and darkness and mystery, Job cannot let go his trust in God. Brought, as it might seem that he was, almost to the point of abandoning it, the strength of that trust only becomes more conspicuous from the strain to which it has been subjected. By its powerful recoil it carries him suddenly back from the verge of the abyss to the immovable foundation. The faith that seemed to be vanishing, if it had not already vanished, rises unexpectably superior over all the tumult of his soul, and all depressing circumstances. From his frantic outcry against the injustice that is slaying him, he passes to the instant expression of his unabated trust in God. *"Surely even now my witness is in heaven, And my evidence is on high. My friends scorn me; My eyes pour out tears to God"* (Job 16:19-20). Job pleads with God, who alone can be his defense and his Redeemer. All others have deserted him. All others misunderstand his character and misinterpret his condition. God is his only refuge. But, under the returning sense of his misery and approaching end, he sinks once more at the close of his speech into a cheerless and despondent frame.

But the victory for which he has been struggling is now near at hand. The elements of hope, which have been gathering in his soul, have attained a consistency which will make them superior in the strife. And his trust in God is preparing to assert itself invincibly, though deprived of all external supports and in the face of all opposition from outward sense.

The more particular examination of the language of his triumph will occupy another chapter.

Now unto Him that kept Job from falling, and who is able likewise to keep us from falling, and to present us faultless before the presence of His glory with exceeding joy, to the only wise God our Savior be glory and majesty, dominion and power, both now and forever. Amen.

CHAPTER 5: COMPREHENSION QUESTIONS

Job's Conflict

1. What did the author mean when he stated that Job's triumph was the triumph of faith over common sense?

2. Faith is sometimes described as hope and confidence strengthened. How did Job show, by his actions, that he had eternal confidence in the Lord? (~~Insert~~ Poem Pg127)

3. Read Hebrews 12:1-11. How might this passage comfort the heart of someone in Job's position?

4. Why is it important for ~~Christians~~ Jews to have a fixed conclusion in their soul that God is truly their friend?

5. Job's tremendous faith permits him to maintain his love for God even though he is unable to comprehend why the Lord acts the way He does. Why does Christian faith require that we trust God even though we cannot fully comprehend the works or nature of God?

6. What does the triumph of Job teach us regarding the sufficiency of God to save without the aid of men or physical instruments?

7. Read Hebrews 4:14-16. How might these verses have helped Job understand that God is so loving that He is willing to lower himself to minister to the needs of his people?

8. How has your appreciation for God's Word grown as you realize how much comforting knowledge you have compared to poor Job?

9. What does the word soliloquy mean?

Chapter 6

Job's Redeemer Triumphs Over Satan

For I know that my Redeemer lives, And He shall stand at last on the earth; And after my skin is destroyed, this I know, That in my flesh I shall see God, Whom I shall see for myself, And my eyes shall behold, and not another. How my heart yearns within me! Job 19:25-27

Job's triumphant assertion of his unshaken confidence in God, which he reaches near the close of the nineteenth chapter, is deservedly ranked as the most important comment in all his speeches. In some respects it is one of the most significant passages in the entire Old Testament, not so much in the positive amount of information which it contains as in the spirit of an unconquerable faith which it discloses. It nearly exalts the patriarch of Uz to the level of the patriarch from Ur, the acknowledged father of the faithful, and marks Job as another conspicuous example of the pattern of faith found in Abraham—the one as distinguished and heroic in his steadfastness in suffering as the other in his unswerving obedience.

The central position of Job's noble comment has been referred to before and is referred to again because it is the turning-point in his discussions with his friends. It is indeed the crowning victory over Satan's fiercest and most subtle temptation. It is faith planting itself firmly on the unseen, when not one single external ground of support remains. The spokes of his anchor have taken hold of the immovable Rock of Ages, and the rage of the tempest and the dashing waves and the heaving sea cannot tear his vessel from its moorings. Held by the strong grasp of the invisible, which is no less real, solid and abiding because it is out of sight, he can safely defy all that is visible and on the surface. Satan's most furious assaults have no power to dislodge him or unsettle his sure and well-grounded persuasion.

The suffering patriarch is, to all human appearance and in his own estimation, sinking rapidly to the grave under an accumulation of disasters which seem to exhaust Satan's fiendish ingenuity of torture, and which appear to involve God's displeasure. His friends charge that God is bearing testimony against his aggravated criminality. Conscious of his integrity, and yet confounded by these apparent evidences of God's hostility to him, he piteously pleads with God to no longer treat him as a criminal. He does not deserve to be so treated. Rather he asks that God's heavy hand be removed, that He bear witness to his innocence and uprightness. But his cries are unanswered. He cannot get his case before the supreme Judge of all so as to obtain the hearing to which he makes his appeal. The Most High does not in any way interfere to clear his name, or to redress the wrongs which His servant is enduring. The heavens are silent. The situation remains unchanged. The sufferings of Job are unabated. His friends continue to taunt him with this plain evidence of guilt.

We have observed the growing intensity of Job's inward struggle, and the strife is not yet relieved. He repels the insinuations of his friends. He rejects their conclusion, for it is contradicted by his own mind and heart. But he cannot properly explain the logic of God's judgments. As a consequence he is tossed by conflicting emotions. He seems to be stuck with the conclusion that God is unrighteously oppressing him, afflicting him without cause, or punishing him for crimes which he has not committed. And if God is unrighteous, then He is not a God to be worshipped and confided in. If he admits this, he has fallen before the temptation and Satan has gained the victory. But how can Job escape it? The facts stare him sternly in the face. And even if he were disposed to shut his eyes to them, his friends would zealously heap upon him their inevitable deductions.

It is a time of outspoken frankness in which the convictions of his soul utter themselves without reserve and without disguise. He cannot shelter himself behind conventional phrases which may have a religious sound, though emptied of their meaning and not expressive of his real and honest faith. He is not in a mood to save appearances by the gloss of pious professions. He dare not deceive himself and others by uncandidly smoothing over difficulties in the divine administration, and persuading himself that he has explained what he has simply evaded. His whole soul is opened before us down to its inmost depths, and his most secret imaginings. He is engaged in a contest for life or death, in which everything is involved, and no mere pretending or flimsy excuses can deliver him. He must have truth on which he can rest with unshaken conviction. He cannot comfort his soul by shallow or insincere declarations.

In the unshrinking truthfulness with which he utters his inmost feelings, we are startled sometimes by the boldness and seeming irreverence with which he evaluates the works of God. But it is not the daring recklessness of idle speculation. Nor is it the profane speech of the wicked blaspheming his Maker. It is the transparent sincerity of the tempted soul, driven almost to distraction by suggestions which are forced upon him, and which he cannot shut out. They are not cherished thoughts on which he loves to dwell and to which he gladly reverts. They are like frightful images from which he shrinks away, but which continue nevertheless to glare upon him until by the surpassing energy of faith the dreadful spell is broken, and the temptation vanquished.

In his former speeches Job has been struggling desperately with the idea perpetually thrust upon him by his friends, and forcing itself upon him from all that he endured, that God was his enemy. Rays of hope have arisen within him, but they have not been sufficient to lift the burden off his heart. In the beginning of this speech he is still oppressed by these evident tokens of God's antagonism. But the argument of guilt deduced from it by his friends he firmly rejects. It is not true, as they urge, that he deserves what he suffers. It is not true that this is a display of divine justice! No, it is injustice! He says, *"If indeed you magnify yourselves against me, And plead my disgrace against me, Know then that God has wronged me..."* (Job 19:5-6). It is the very word that Bildad had used in a former address, in his pious indignation at the sentiments of Job, *"Does God subvert judgment? Or does the Almighty pervert justice?"* (Job 8:3). And it is the same that Elihu uses subsequently in his rebuke of Job's rash and impatient utterances, *"Surely God will not do wickedly, Nor will the Almighty pervert justice"* (Job 34:12).

But such perversion Job boldly affirms to exist in his own case. He denies the justice of executing sentence upon him for crimes of which he was free. If God, in sending these sufferings upon him, has marked him out as a criminal, as his friends allege, then He has perverted justice; He has done him wrong. He adds, *"If I cry out concerning wrong, I am not heard. I cry aloud, there is no justice"* (Job 19:7). He is the innocent victim of most cruel treatment. He is the defenseless subject of ruffianly violence who screams for help against pitiless and inhuman outrage, who calls for justice against the most grievous oppression and wrong. But his cries are uttered in vain. No help is given him. There is no relaxation of the extreme of injury inflicted. And he proceeds with his harrowing recital of these causeless and intense inflictions: *"He has fenced up my way so that I cannot pass, And He has set darkness in my paths. He has stripped me of my glory, And taken the crown from my head. He breaks me down on every side, And I am gone; My hope He has uprooted like a tree. He has also kindled His wrath against me, And He counts me as one of His enemies. His troops come together And build up their road against me; They encamp all around my tent"* (Job 19:8-12). My brothers, acquaintances, kinsfolk, familiar friends, my servants, and my very wife—everyone I have loved has turned against me. *"My bone clings to my skin and to my flesh, And I have escaped by the skin of my teeth. Have pity on me, have pity upon me, O my friends, For the hand of God has struck me. Why do you persecute me as God does, And are not satisfied with my flesh?"* (Job 19:20-22) Why will you too join in this relentless persecution which God has initiated against me, and which can only be compared to savage beasts of prey tearing and gnawing my flesh with a greed that cannot be satisfied?

Against such cruelty and injustice on the part of both God and man he enters his earnest protest, and he would have his words put on permanent record. Outcast alike from God and man, he makes his appeal to the rocks. Let the enduring rock be his monumental witness. Let there be carved there, in letters that shall not fade, the inscription of his innocence. Though God and man combine to condemn him, let his own statements of his integrity be engraved with an iron pen, and be filled in with lead in the rock forever. And thus may the everlasting rocks, in legible inscriptions never to be effaced, bear testimony on his behalf. And may the justice that he vainly craves find at least its indelible record there.

It is customary to understand Job here as saying that he would have the words which immediately follow engraved in the rock. He would have that golden sentence, *"I know that my Redeemer lives, etc."* stand on perpetual record, his legacy to future ages, his testimony through all time that, forsaken as he seemed to be by God and man, he never gave up his confident trust in God his Savior. In his last and darkest hours he still held fast his unwavering assurance that God was his Redeemer and Friend, and though his body perished and crumbled into dust, he would still with his own eyes see God who would appear on his behalf. And if any prefer so to interpret the patriarch's wish, we make no serious objection. These words are certainly worthy of being recorded on the solid rock. No grander monumental inscription can be found. Job could not have a worthier epitaph upon his rock-hewn tomb. In no way could a more exalted testimony be rendered to his steadfast piety than by preserving this outburst of triumphant faith, uttered under such circumstances. These words stand out conspicuously upon the speeches of Job, as the noblest, the loftiest, the most supreme that he ever uttered, and the most aptly significant of the power of his Savior and the reality of his pious trust in God.

Yet it seems to us that those interpreters have more accurately perceived Job's own meaning who think that he would have in lasting record on the rock, not the particular statement about to be made, but the things he said, the assertions of his innocence which had appeared in his previous speeches. Job's desire to have his words inscribed upon the rock is not so much an introduction to what he is about to declare in his strong declaration, as rather the conclusion of what precedes. It does not represent his rising consciousness of triumph, but rather his lowest depth of desolation and hopeless despair, joined with his inward consciousness of integrity that demands some recognition. Destitute of every human helper and crushed beneath an unrighteous sentence, his appeals to God unheard, he asks that the rocks may take up his dying declaration. He desires that his words may be indelibly written there so that the imperishable stone may speak of his innocence in the face of false charges and testify of the wrong that has been done him after his own voice is gone. And so his appeal to the rocks to transmit his defense to all coming time will be parallel to his passionate reference to the earth in his last speech, *"O earth, do not cover my blood, And let my cry have no resting place"* (16:18). It is the outcry of one hopelessly overwhelmed by wrongful treatment, one to whom his integrity is dearer than his life, and one who insists that what is true and right shall have the assertion to which it is entitled. Here is one who cannot but believe after all, that eternal justice shall find a response somewhere and at some time. What is right and just must be clarified!

This view of these words is confirmed by the form of Job's triumphant declaration which follows. This is not a separate, disconnected sentence, as though it were framed to be inscribed by itself upon the rock. But it is intimately linked with what precedes, as though it had been intended not to stand alone, but to form part of a continuous context, beginning as it does with a conjunction. *"For I know,"* or, more strictly rendered, *"And I know that my Redeemer lives."* A monumental inscription could not begin with 'and'. This necessarily marks a connection with some thought either expressed or implied in what precedes. And this connection or continuation, while it would be strange as an isolated statement on the rocks, is readily understood within the context just explained.

Perishing under groundless accusations of whose falsity he is profoundly conscious, but which he has no means of adequately refuting, he utters as his last wish—even while the grave is opening before him—that this amount of justice may be done him, to place his statement of innocence on record in the rock. And as he utters the wish, the certainty that justice must stand flashes in his soul with strong conviction, "I have asked a record on the rock; and all the while I know that my Redeemer lives. I need no monument of stone to vindicate me, no inscription engraved with an iron pen and filled in with letters of molten lead. I have an ever-living and almighty Redeemer who will rescue me from wrong and defend me as a friend. Therefore, I will with implicit confidence entrust my cause to Him."

There cannot be a moment's doubt as to the identity of the Redeemer that Job is trusting to rescue him. It is the same of whom he spoke in his last speech, "... *My witness is in heaven, and my record is on high*" (Job 16:19). This is the One he had begged to be his deliverer when all others refused to take up his cause. Again and again he had expressed his strong assurance that if his cause could be brought before Him, then the sentence would be in his favor. Now all doubts have vanished. Every condition that had previously clogged his hopes is removed. The Lord has undertaken for him. The Lord has engaged upon his side. The Lord will defend him against all injury and wrong. God, who seems to be persecuting him with such relentless hostility is not his enemy—He is his Redeemer.

It is commonly supposed, and with reason, that in this word 'redeemer' there lies an allusion to an institution dating from the simple and as yet but partially regulated society of patriarchal times, and which was subsequently admitted with some restrictions and modifications into the Mosaic code. It was the formal duty of the next of kin to take up the cause of his injured or impoverished relative. He was to redeem his property, restore it to him if he, in any way, forfeited it or had been obliged to sell it. He was to defend him against injury and wrong; especially, he was to avenge his blood if he had been unrighteously slain. Now God has assumed the part of the next kinsman in relation to Job. He shall redress his wrongs and avenge his injuries. He shall deliver him out of the bondage of his sorrows (this figure appears later in this book, when the Lord is said to have *"turned the captivity of Job."*) The frequency with which the title of Redeemer is applied to God in the Old Testament makes still plainer its application here. Jacob speaks of the divine Angel that redeemed him from all evil (Gen. 48:16). Moses sings of the people that God has redeemed (Exod. 15:13). David invokes the Lord, his strength and his redeemer (Ps. 19:14). With Isaiah, it is a favorite name: The Redeemer, the Lord of hosts, who is first and who is last (Isa. 44:6).

When Job expresses his assurance that his Redeemer lives, he means not merely that he now exists (as opposed to the idea that there is no one now existing who can appreciate his case and understand his real character, and who is willing to deliver him). Nor is it simply meant that He possesses a conscious existence in contrast with the lifeless, insensate rock so that, Job is not limited to the mute testimony carved upon the motionless, unconscious stone. He has a living witness and personal defender. The true Redeemer exhibits active agency as a natural part of his character—as when the Lord is styled the living God in contrast with the dead and lifeless idols, who are of no service to their worshippers. The living God is a God who has power to save and to destroy and who exerts His power as the occasion demands. A living Redeemer is one who is more than a powerful force or a name. He is one who will act with real substantial effect. His eye is on the sparrow.

The rest of Job's triumphant testimony, as it appears in the King James Version, would lead us to suppose that Job expected his vindication to be postponed until the end of the world and the general resurrection. It runs: *"For I know that my Redeemer lives, And He shall stand at last on the earth; and after my skin is destroyed, this I know, That in my flesh I shall see God"* (Job 19:25-26).

Our translators have here followed older versions. And without designing to warp the meaning of Job or to change the intent of his words, they have been unconsciously guided in the sense which they have assigned to his expressions by their knowledge of doctrines subsequently revealed with a clearness greater than that with which they had been made known in the time of Job, or with which they are here presented to his own mind.

Job is speaking under strong excitement, and in the language of lofty poetry. He uses no superfluous words. He simply indicates his meaning in the most concise manner, without rounding out his periods or using those connectives and significant particles which would be demanded in complicated prose. So his sentences are abrupt and elliptical, and exactness of translation is difficult. The embarrassment of the English translators is shown by the unusual number of words supplied—and these are of no small importance to the meaning. There are a few grammatical questions in the original passage which it is difficult to settle with absolute certainty, but which, however determined, do not materially affect the general sense. Without laying any stress upon these, therefore, we propose the following rendering as sufficiently accurate for our present purpose: *"And I know my Redeemer lives, and last on earth shall He arise; and after my skin, which has been destroyed thus, and out of my flesh shall I see God."*

He does not say that his Redeemer shall stand upon the earth or make His appearance on it, but that He shall arise, and take action. He shall no longer sit still, as though He were not concerned or were disposed to take no part in what was happening. He shall arise and participate actively. This is similar to when the suffering Psalmists so often call upon God to arise: *"Arise, O Lord! Save me, O my God!"* (Psalm 3:7). *"Arise, O Lord! Let not man prevail"!* (Psalm 9:19). *"Arise for our help, and redeem us for Thy mercies' sake"* (Psalm 44:26).

He shall arise last on earth, here spoken of as the scene of the conflict and the trials which He is to terminate and rectify. Or, as the words may mean, and some able interpreters with a measure of plausibility understand them to mean, 'over the dust.' The dust, that is, into which my body has meanwhile mouldered away. Upon which rendering there would be a distinct assertion of what was already, perhaps involved in the term 'last,' and what is more fully brought out in the words that follow, that this intervention of his great Redeemer shall occur after he is dead. It will not take place until his body shall have been committed to the grave and mouldered back to dust.

But whether this meaning be expressed in this particular phrase or not, it is made distinctly prominent in what follows, *"And after my skin is destroyed, this I know, That in my flesh I shall see God."* He looks to a period after the destruction, the complete disintegration of his skin. And when he himself, the living part, the vital spirit, shall be separated from his flesh, his decaying and lifeless body—that will be the time he looks to. The just sense of these expressions compels us to regard Job as contemplating the time after he shall be dead, and affirming that then his Redeemer God shall manifest Himself to his disembodied spirit.

Another interpretation which has been put upon this verse, and upon this whole passage, conceives Job to be here looking forward not to a future state, but to the restoration of God's favor, and his own deliverance out of all his troubles in this present life. This is not wholly a modern view, nor has it been confined to unbelieving interpreters. On the contrary, it was adopted by some of the most eminent of the Christian Fathers, and has been ably advocated both in ancient and in recent times. The decisive objections to it are:

1.   It does not give their fair meaning to the expressions just recited, which must denote something more than a skin damaged and a body emaciated by disease. It is something posterior to the total destruction and dissolution of the body that is referred to.

2.   This is further evident from the constant tenor of Job's language elsewhere. He regards himself as on the verge of the grave, which is already claiming him as its own (16:16) Every temporal prospect has vanished. He invariably repels the idea of any improvement of his condition in this world as plainly impossible, and as though the very suggestion of it were an insult to his understanding. He cannot, therefore, himself anticipate what he uniformly pronounces irrational and absurd.

3.   The same thing appears from the general drift of his argument with his friends, both prior to this passage and subsequent to it. His friends affirm that men are rewarded or punished in this life according to their characters. Job generally denies it. If he here utters his expectation that God will interfere to reward his piety in the present life, he largely abandons his own position and adopts theirs.

4.   It very materially lowers the evidence and the power of Job's faith, if we suppose him to be referring to the present life. The victory which he here gains, and which assures his triumph over Satan's temptation—over every possible temptation—is the victory of faith over outward sense. If any possible hope were left him in this world, the triumph would be less conspicuous and complete. It is only when we see him shut up absolutely to the unseen and see that with his trust in God he ventures boldly into it, not groping blindly or bewildered as in the dark, not hesitating as in uncertainty or perplexity, not shrinking as from possible danger or mistake, but confident as if treading on solid ground, that we discern the true heroism of a faith like that of Job and its unconquerable energy. In his own esteem he is sinking into the grave with every indication surrounding him of God's relentless hostility. Every possibility of a return to God's favor in this life is, to his mind, utterly shut out. And yet so fixed is he in his inward persuasion of the real friendship and redeeming grace of God to him, he bursts the boundaries of time, passes the limits of the visible and the tangible, and knows that the manifest tokens of the divine love, which are denied him here, will be granted to him there. What can shake the trust or destroy the peace of that man who rests his certain hope on the immutable attributes of God? Satan and the world may vent their rage and ply their arts against him in vain. He is proof against every assault, for his

steadfast trust is founded upon the eternal rock, and this is a foundation which never can be shaken.

It is no real objection to the view which has been taken of this passage that, in the final stages of the history of Job, God actually did interfere for the delivery of His servant and the restoration of his prosperity in the present life. What was in the secret purpose and plan of God must be carefully distinguished from Job's situation as it appeared to his own mind. It was the fact of his being left so entirely in the dark, and without the slightest clue as to the design or issue of his sufferings, that created all the mystery, laid such demands on his faith, and established such a searching test of the reality and power of his adherence to God's service. God did indeed remove Job's sorrows, renewing to him the open pledges of His favor in this life. He thus rewarded His servant's faith, contrary to and beyond all expectation. Job never dreamed of such a result, as all his speeches show.

Nor is there impressive force in the objection that Job has in his previous speeches uniformly spoken of death as the end of every activity and hope, and has never let fall a syllable from which it could be inferred that he believed in the reality and certainty of a future state. The conclusion has hence been drawn that this cannot have been an article of his faith, and that he could not therefore have referred to it in the passage now under consideration. But this is to overlook entirely the progress in Job's own mind which is delineated in such a vigorous and masterly manner in the course of his speeches. We see Job in the beginning involved in all the mist and obscurity which overhung the future state in the patriarchal age, when no clear revelations had been made upon this subject. The continued conscious existence of the soul was known, but all was vague and shadowy in regard to that other life. Job is, by the intensity of the struggle in which he was engaged, driven step by step into clearer views of this subject than he possessed before. We can watch his clumsy advances toward it, and his stirring teachings that prevail. And here we see him desperately trying to grasp the unseen hand of God as the only way out of inextricable darkness and despair. He was led by the unseen God to the only resting place for his wavering soul—the immutable grace of God, which nothing can wrest from him. It seems to him, however, that there is no room remaining for God's favor to display itself to him in this world. And the imperative necessity of his holiest and firmest convictions compels him to the declaration, "I know that God will manifest His favor to me, though it be after my body has decayed and my spirit has flown away."

Nor is there any greater weight in the additional objection that Job makes no further use of this great truth in his controversy with his friends. He never refers to it subsequently, whether to console himself under the rigors of his own hard lot, or to shed light on the enigmas of Providence in the unequal distribution of good and evil, or to refute the constantly repeated tenet of his friends of a retribution in the present life. A doctrine of such vast importance in its bearings on the subject under discussion could not, it is alleged, flash up in one single passage and then never be alluded to again. The fact that it is not brought up and insisted upon elsewhere is believed by some to signify that it is not really here.

But this is to mistake entirely the part which this doctrine plays in the book of Job. It is not offered as a solution for the enigmas of divine Providence. It is not even presented as the basis of consolation for the tempted and afflicted. The comfort of the sorrowing rests on a deeper ground than this, as is subsequently unfolded in the speech of Elihu, and by the Lord Himself, to whom it is reserved to present in its true light a subject which has only been growing more and more perplexed under the reasonings and discussions of Job and his three friends. The doctrine of immortality comes in solely to still Job's inward conflict, and bring him to a settled conviction that there is peace between his soul and God, which no outward and temporal troubles can destroy. This it effectually does. Job's inward agitation ceases to overwhelm him. He is no longer devastated by the sense of God's hostility and wrath. His outward situation is unchanged, and the problem of his sufferings is as mysterious as ever. But he has attained to inward peace. He knows that his Redeemer lives, and that, after his worn and suffering body shall be resolved into dust, the clouds shall break away, which now obstruct his vision of the face of God. The lesson of immortality has accomplished its end. It need not, therefore, be repeated. And that it is not applied to matters with which in the plan and purpose of this book it has nothing to do, is surely no argument against its appearance here, where its revelation was essential.

But in what relation, it may be further asked, does this passage stand to the doctrine of the Messiah and of a corporeal resurrection? Is Job's Redeemer ours? Is his faith the same in which the people of God now rejoice in the completed victory over death and the grave? In germ and substance it was, but, as it lay before his consciousness, not in the same developed form. God was his Redeemer: Christ, who was in the beginning with God and was God, is ours. When Job appeals to his Redeemer, he does so without even apprehending that He is the second person of the Godhead. He knew nothing of the distinction of persons in the divine Being, and of the doctrine of the Trinity as fully unfolded in the New Testament. But he addresses Him in a character and solicits the fulfillment of an office which distinctively belongs to God the Son. He is, and has been in every age, the Redeemer out of every distress, the Guardian and Protector of His people, and their Deliverer both from temporal distress and from that everlasting woe of which the former is the figure and example. It is He to whom the saints of God are indebted for that joyful prospect of the vision of God beyond the grave to which Job looked forward. In this regard, the doctrine of Christ is here approached from its divine side, not as Abraham's son, but as God's.

And then perhaps it may not be without its deeper significance and its divinely intended meaning that the term Redeemer had the association linked with it, both in patriarchal and Mosaic usage, of the next of kin. Is there not here possibly a foreshadowing of more than Job himself intended or imagined when he used the word? It may well be the intent of God to point us to that divine Redeemer, who is after all our nearest Kinsman, and who allied Himself to us in the bonds of our common humanity, bone of our bone and flesh of our flesh, that He might have a kinsman's right to take up our cause. Christ, our Elder Brother, vindicates us from the accusations of the law, and frees us from the sentence of death written in our members, and opens to us life and immortality with His work on the cross. As Abraham saw Christ's day, it may likewise be said of Job that he rejoiced to see Christ's day, and he saw it and was glad.

The human aspect of Christ's work, so far as it is foreshown in the book of Job, is primarily set forth by Job himself, in his own person, as the type of the man of sorrows, forsaken and persecuted by his friends, and abandoned apparently by God, and yet for whom the cross was the passage way to the crown. Like Christ, Job's suffering had a glorious reward. The fruit of Job's tribulations abounded to the blessing of others, as Job's intercession also brought healing to his three friends, and he has been a helper to the distressed from his own day to the present.

The resurrection of the body was probably not present to Job's thoughts, certainly not in the form of a general and simultaneous rising from the dead. And yet it is so linked, generally at least, with our continued spiritual existence that it is natural and even necessary for us to transfer our ideas of being, drawn from the present state, to the great hereafter. It may perhaps be truly said that the germs of the doctrine of the resurrection may likewise be detected here. Job says, *"Whom I shall see for myself, and my eyes shall behold, and not another"* so natural was it to transfer the thought of those physical organs of sight along with this personal identity, even while speaking of himself as disembodied. We shall not here revive the curious and profitless speculation to which these words have given rise, nor shall we involve ourselves in any discussion as to whether Job means eyes of the soul or eyes of the body. It is enough that we find here suggested the intimacy of the link which binds the two parts of our nature together, and the powerful association which almost inevitably carries us forward from the continued life of the soul to the restored life of the body.

Our souls and bodies are sown in corruption, but they will be raised in incorruption.

CHAPTER 6: COMPREHENSION QUESTIONS

Job's Redeemer Triumphs Over Satan

1. What did the writer believe that Job and Abraham had in common?

2. Why did the author feel that Job's statements in chapter nineteen, verses twenty-five through twenty-seven, were a turning point in the conflict he was facing?

3. Learning to wait on God for answers to prayer is never easy. Why was it especially difficult for Job?

4. Do you believe that the Lord was upset with Job because he spoke so boldly and frankly before him during his miseries?

5. In what manner do Christians sometimes try to mask their true feelings by the way they choose their words?

6. In those cases in which Job openly speculates as to whether God's standard of justice is proper, do you think that Job was speaking wisely? Please explain your answer.

7. The Bible states that, "to whom much has been given, much will be required." What bearing does this principle have as it relates to Job?

8. Do you think that Job was too pre-occupied with his effort to declare his innocence or do you think it was a legitimate priority? Please explain your answer.

9. In what sense was Job like the Savior, Jesus Christ?

10. Is it likely that Job had a clear understanding of the Godhead or of the doctrine of the bodily resurrection of the dead?

Chapter 7

Job Refutes His Friends

"How then can you comfort me with empty words, Since falsehood remains in your answers?" —Job 21:34

The crisis of the temptation is past, but Job's perplexity is not yet removed. He refuses to be driven from his constant trust in God by all the influences that Satan has arrayed against him. Amidst all the seeming evidences of God's hostility, he maintains his confidence in him as his Redeemer. He who is afflicting him now will effect his deliverance hereafter. But the time of this deliverance has not yet come. He is walking in darkness, trusting in the Lord.

Until now Job has spoken principally to God. It was with Him that he had to do, rather than with his friends. That which has been chiefly agitating him, and which was in fact the mainspring of the temptation, was the question of his personal relation to his Maker. When his friends affirmed and reiterated, as they did in every speech they made, that it was the wicked who suffered under God's righteous rule and in proportion to their wickedness, Job made immediate application of this, as they designed that he should, to his own case. He had, indeed, more than once declared the falsity of the general principle, *"... He destroys the blameless and the wicked. If the scourge slays suddenly, He laughs at the plight of the innocent. The earth is given into the hand of the wicked. He covers the faces of its judges"* (Job 9:22-24). *"The tents of robbers prosper, And those who provoke God are secure—In what God provides by His hand"* (Job 12:6).

But this was only incidental to the main current of his thoughts. He was in no mood for an abstract discussion. The personal question involved in it swallowed up every other consideration. It concerned what was dearer to him than life. It affected the very foundation of his trust in God. It was not simply that he had a tender regard for his reputation, and that he could not bear to have a cloud brought over his good name.

80

He who had borne the loss of property and children and endured the sufferings inflicted on his own person with such noble resignation could also have properly submitted to false reproaches. That was not the tenderest and most vital point. The estimation in which he was held by his fellow-men was not his chief treasure. But his conscious integrity was an inalienable possession. This he could not part with. And if what his friends said was true, as the actions of Him who ruled the world seemed to support, then God was punishing him for crimes which he was conscious that he had never committed. He was, indeed, in a most pitiable dilemma. If he denied the position of his friends, then the plain inference was that God was unjust. If he assented to it, then God was unjust. And, in either case, how could he serve a God who was unjust or cruel?

Satan at last seemed to have driven him into a position from which there was no escape. How can he do otherwise than renounce the service of God? What basis remains for that confidence and reverential homage which is essential to true worship? Satan has completely surrounded him with his deadly snare, and it would appear as though there were no alternative. Job must fall before his adversary.

We have traced the fierce and weary conflict to its final issue. We have watched him in his inward strife, in his piteous moans, his declarations to God, his vain appeals to Him to declare Himself on his side. We have seen him driven to and fro in his tumultuous agitation until, forced to the very edge of the precipice and apparently about to fall hopelessly into the awful pit that opened beneath him, he cleared it by one energetic act of faith. The gift of faith enabled Job to hold on to God without visible support.

The personal question is now largely settled, and his intense inward agitation has subsided. He is in a calmer and more tranquil state of mind. He has gained that unshaken conviction of the rectitude and goodness of God which enables him to claim Him as his Redeemer in spite of all adverse appearances. This source of his turmoil is put to rest. The power of the temptation is broken. Satan cannot detach him from the service of God, since he holds fast to his faith in Him in spite of all the suggestions of sense and of reason.

Job is safe from falling. But outward sense and human reason still present a problem which baffles him completely. He holds fast to his confidence in God, but he is bewildered nevertheless. The solution of his friends is no solution. According to their principles, indeed, there is nothing but predictable Providence. They see nothing but the uniform reign of God's justice. Job shows, on the contrary, that this is not the case. He takes issue with them in regard to their fundamental principle and exposes its error. It is not, as they allege, a fact of uniform experience that the righteous are rewarded and the wicked suffer. This is the point to which he addresses himself in his remaining speeches.

It is, as he says, a most distressing truth, one that fills him with painful emotions at every contemplation of it and at which they might well stand amazed themselves. The administration of this world is not conducted on such evident principles of equity as they have maintained. *"Look at me and be astonished; Put your hand over your mouth. Even when I remember I am terrified, And trembling takes hold of my flesh."* (Job 21:5, 6). So far from just retribution overtaking the guilty, bad men are often particularly prospered. *"Why do the wicked live and become old, Yes, become mighty in power? Their descendants are established with them in their sight, And their offspring before their eyes. Their houses are safe from fear, Neither is the rod of God upon them. Their bull breeds without failure; Their cow calves without miscarriage. They send forth their little ones like a flock, and their children dance. They sing to the tambourine and harp, And rejoice to the sound of the flute. They spend their days in wealth, And in a moment go down to the grave"* (Job 21:7-13). Their merry, joyous prosperity continues to the very last. Experiencing no unusual calamity, with no check upon their good fortune and no term of suffering that could be regarded as a penalty for their misdeeds, they go down peacefully and quietly to the grave. Their life is filled up with pleasure and with every form of earthly good to its very close. And the natural consequence follows. In their arrogant and foolish presumption they refuse all subjection to the Most High. *"Yet they say to God, 'Depart from us, for we do not desire the knowledge of Your ways. Who is the Almighty, that we should serve Him? And what profit do we have if we pray to Him?'"* (Job 21:14, 15)

Bildad had said, *"The light of the wicked indeed goes out,"* and, *"Destruction is ready at his side"* (Job 18:5,12). Job asks in reply, How often is this the case? It is by no means the invariable rule. *"How often is the lamp of the wicked put out? How often does their destruction come upon them, The sorrows God distributes in His anger? They are like straw before the wind, And like chaff that a storm carries away."* (Job 21:17, 18).

But, declare the friends, the retribution is sure to come. It is only delayed awhile. *"God lays up his iniquity for his children"* (Job 5:4; Job

82

18:18; Job 20:10). This, Job retorts is no retribution at all in any proper sense. *"Let Him reward him,"* (that is, the sinner himself, in his own person) *that he may know it. Let his eyes see his destruction, and let him drink of the wrath of the Almighty. For what pleasure does he have in his house after him, when the number of his months is cut off in the midst?"* How is he affected by what happens to his children after he is dead and gone? They were presuming to *"teach God knowledge"* by thus prescribing a law for His government of the world, and might justly fear that sentence with which He rewards the proud. On the other hand, he alleges that in actual fact there was no discrimination exercised in the fortunes allotted to men. No reason could be assigned why some men never have trouble, and others never have anything else. *"You say, Where is the house of the prince? and where are the dwelling-places of the wicked?"* (implying that they have disappeared, or that their ruins only remain as monuments of God's righteous vengeance—but this is not so). Ungodly men are often screened from calamities that befall better men. And when they die, instead of being regarded as wicked, cut off by the just sentence of Heaven, they are buried with every mark of distinction, attendant crowds doing honor to their memory and evil example.

Astounded by this forceful attack upon their stronghold, this direct denial of what they have all along been asserting as an immovable principle, and the foundation of their whole argument, the friends are obliged to modify materially their method of attack. Eliphaz, who speaks next, comes to the rescue of the principle by a furious onslaught on Job himself. Their oft-repeated principle, in its broad universality, cannot again be affirmed in the face of what has just been said. But he is more than ever convinced that it exposes the real secret of all Job's troubles. Whether it can be established as a general rule or not, whether it is applicable to all other cases or not, it unquestionably holds true in this instance. He therefore restricts himself no longer to clever insinuations or indirect suggestions, but makes specific charges of enormous wickedness, and assigns this as the undoubted reason for Job's terrible inflictions. God could have no motive for dealing with Job otherwise than with impartial justice. He must have been guilty, therefore, of atrocious crimes, the righteous penalty for which he is now enduring.

The whole matter is thus brought to a simple issue. Is Job a gross transgressor, or is he not? The charge is direct and unambiguous. Job promptly takes up the challenge and meets the charge with an equally explicit denial. God has indeed hidden Himself in the mystery of these inexplicable sorrows, which continue to press upon Him with the same dire weight as before. He is withdrawn beyond the reach of outward sense. But concealed as He is from sight, impossible as it is to penetrate to His secret seat to urge his plea and to obtain the removal of these distresses under which he now groans, Job yet makes to Him his confident appeal: *"... He knows the way that I take; When He has tested me, I shall come forth as gold. My foot has held fast to His steps; I have kept His way and have not turned aside. I have not departed from the commandment of His lips; I have treasured the words of His mouth more than my necessary food"* (Job 23:10-12). And, as he proceeds to say, the world is full of just such seeming contradictions, of open wickedness that is allowed to go unpunished, and of grievous wrongs that are not set right.

As the charges brought against Job are wholly destitute of proof, being mere inferences from a principle (which has been shown to be unverified by the actual experience of the world), Bildad cannot again repeat them in the face of Job's solemn declaration of his innocence and his appeal to the Searcher of hearts. There is consequently nothing for him to do, if he would maintain the show of an argument, but to fall back upon the sinfulness inherent in human nature. No man can be pure in the sight of the infinite God. This point had been made by Eliphaz at the very outset of the discussion, and it had been sufficiently answered long since. Bildad, sensible of the weakness of his position, makes no attempt to illustrate or enforce it, and, after a few feebly uttered sentences, relapses into silence. The friends withdraw in frustration from the contest.

Job cannot refrain from taunting them with the completeness of their failure in an argument which they have been conducting with so much pride. He then seizes the opportunity to guard his language against misconception. In saying what he had done regarding the inequalities of divine providence, he had neither meant to reflect upon the glorious nature of God, nor to deny the existence of moral retributions. He accordingly affirms the exalted majesty of God in as lofty terms as his friends themselves could employ. And though he continues to insist on his own integrity, notwithstanding the afflictions sent upon him, he freely admits the reality of God's providential government, and that punishment does overtake the ungodly. Nevertheless there is a mystery enveloping the divine administration which is quite impenetrable to the human understanding.

This thought of the impossibility of men's arriving at any comprehension of the divine plan in the administration of the universe by their own unaided powers is illustrated with great beauty. A proper example is taken from the art of mining. Men can discover the precious and useful metals, though they are hidden deep underground. They will descend into the bowels of the earth and push their shafts remote from the habitation of men. Regardless of the obstructions that block their way, and of the gathering streams that hinder their progress, and of the obscurity which reigns in these dark abysses, they cut a passage through the rocks to the treasures which they seek. But there is a greater treasure by far, which cannot be obtained in this way—a treasure that gold or silver cannot equal, and which vastly exceeds in worth the most valuable jewels and precious stones. This can never be discovered by the searching or by the ingenuity of men. Where shall wisdom be found? Where is the place of understanding? It is hidden from the eyes of all living. Even the world of the departed does not possess it. They have heard the fame of it, but they are not able to grasp it. There is but one Being in the universe who does possess a perfect comprehension of God's grand plan, and that is He who adjusted all things with infinite precision, He who is guiding all to His own preordained results. And He who is infinite in knowledge has disclosed to man wherein true practical wisdom lies— *"God understands its way, And He knows its place. For He looks to the ends of the earth, And sees under the whole heavens, To establish a weight for the wind, And mete out the waters by measure. When He made a law for the rain, And a path for the thunderbolt, Then He saw wisdom and declared it; He prepared it, indeed He searched it out. And to man He said, 'Behold, the fear of the Lord that is wisdom, And to depart from evil is understanding.' "* (Job 28:23-28)

Start Here

The providence of God is not conducted upon such a predictable rule, and one so perfectly simple and susceptible of easy application, as the friends have maintained. The dealings of the infinite God are not regulated on a principle so obvious as to be level to the humblest understanding. On the contrary, they are enveloped in the profoundest mystery. It is impossible to lift the veil which obscures His designs or to penetrate the reasons which govern the divine proceedings. This is not because there is no reason in them. The impossibility of discovering the divine order does not arise from the absence of any real order in the universe. The world is not under the dominion of chance, swinging to and fro at random without intelligent oversight. Our world is not a ship without compass or rudder, tossed by the waves and driven by the winds. Nor is it under the blind sway of inexorable 'fate.' Nor has it been surrendered to the mere control of physical laws, working out their fixed and uniform sequences with a relentless disregard for anything but inherent material properties, which with undeviating precision pursue each their own affinities without owning a superintending control or a subordination to high moral aims. Nor is the Ruler of the universe a capricious tyrant whose absolute power is directed by mere arbitrary will, without wise forethought or well-considered purpose.

Infinite wisdom reigns through the universe. The same Lord who adjusted the physical forces of external nature with such admirable precision, who balanced their action with such delicate skill, also insures that no derangement ensues in the onward movement of all this complicated machinery through successive ages. He who established and perpetuates this universal harmony in all material things, giving their weight to the winds and their measure to the waters, orders with equal wisdom the numerous affairs of men. There is a divine method. There is an infinite plan. And it is one that is worthy of the supreme Intelligence. It bears throughout the stamp of consummate wisdom. This wisdom is, however, by its very nature beyond the understanding of finite creatures.

We cannot attain to a comprehension of all the wisdom of God. We cannot see how its several parts blend with each other, or how they consist with the perfections of Him who designed it and who is conducting it. There is much that, to human view, seems to be at variance with a well-ordered administration. There is much that we cannot account for, much that we cannot understand. There are many things in the management of the world that completely baffle every attempt to unbridle them. We cannot see why they are, nor why God permits them, nor how He can consistently permit them. With our limited understandings and our restricted range of observation, we cannot pretend to fathom the bottomless deep, nor measure what has no bound. We cannot, even by the most prolonged search or the most elaborate investigation, attain to a thorough understanding of God's infinite designs. The mind that resolves all mysteries, harmonizes all strifes, reconciles all contradictions, and reduces everything to perfect order belongs to God alone.

Man can never aspire to a comprehension of the absolute wisdom, but the Most High has mercifully revealed to man all that is necessary for his practical guidance. He may not presume to know how God governs the world, or what rules He prescribes for His own procedure, but he has been sufficiently taught how to direct his own conduct and how to govern his own life. He cannot solve the mysteries of Providence, but he may solve what is of more immediate importance to Him: all questions of personal duty. He cannot tell the end, which is often blocked by everything which God permits or brings to pass. Nevertheless, he does not need to be in doubt as to how he may accomplish the true mission of his own life, how he can secure his own highest welfare. *"The fear of the Lord that is wisdom, And to depart from evil is understanding"* (Job 28:28).

Job pauses here, as he had done once before, waiting to see if his friends had more to say. Whether on account of Job's steadfastness in his own views they think that it will be useless to argue further, or whether they begin themselves to suspect the unsoundness of their position, and to perceive that there is more mystery in the case of their suffering friend than they had imagined—they at any rate say nothing. Job then proceeds to state at length the unsolved nature of his sorrows. His friends have shed no light upon this distressing situation, and he can get none himself. He dwells upon his former happy condition, then recites the dismal set back which he has experienced. Finally, he solemnly affirms his innocence of any crime which could account for his being treated in this way.

The words of Job are here ended. He stands face to face with a mystery that is thus far wholly unexplained. He has no theory, and can imagine none upon which his present sorrows can be accounted for. His friends undertook to silence his complaint, but he has instead silenced them. He holds fast to his faith in God, but he does so notwithstanding the fact that he cannot rid himself of troubling questions that have arisen in his soul. Nor can he align his faith with the facts which he can neither escape nor explain away, those which seem to be directly contrary with the divine attributes. He gloomily says, *"Therefore I am terrified at His presence; When I consider this, I am afraid of Him. For God made my heart weak, And the Almighty terrifies me"*: (Job 23:15, 16). There is an unrest in his soul which he cannot compose. Satan has not been able to destroy him, but he has plunged him into darkness and distress, out of which he cannot find his way. His trust in God continues, however. He still confides in his Redeemer, who after his skin is destroyed and his flesh has mouldered back to dust, will reveal Himself to his disembodied spirit. But will God allow his servant to go on in darkness to the end, bearing his heavy burden, and hoping against hope? Must Job die under the cloud?

Job will soon discover that God sometimes comes in the clouds, and that sometimes our faith can only grow when the Lord's face cannot be found.

CHAPTER 7: COMPREHENSION QUESTIONS

Job Refutes His Friends

1. Did the author believe that Job was deeply concerned and anxious to resolve his problems so his reputation among men could be restored?

2. Does the Bible teach that the godly are always rewarded in this life and the wicked are consistently obliged to suffer?

3. When Job's friends, Eliphaz in particular, fail to convince him of his guilt, what new strategy do they employ to try to break Job's resistance?

4. Can man achieve any genuine comprehension of God's divine administration of the world through his own un-aided powers? Explain your answer.

5. Can we rightly draw from the teachings of the book of Job that our world is under the dominion of chance?

6. Why is it often difficult for people to understand the reasons why our world operates the way it does?

7. Read 1 Cor. 13. What does this passage of Scripture teach concerning when believers are going to be given full understanding of all things?

Chapter 8

Elihu

"Then the wrath of Elihu, the son of Barachel the Buzite, of the family of Ram, was aroused against Job; his wrath was aroused because he justified himself rather than God. Also against his three friends his wrath was aroused, because they had found no answer, and yet had condemned Job." Job 32: 2, 3.

The three friends of Job cannot answer him, and yet it is plain that he ought to be answered. He has silenced his friends, showing that the principle which they have so confidently urged will not explain the mystery of God's dealings in general, nor solve the dilemma of his own case. But he has not brought the question to any satisfactory settlement. The friends undertook to justify God's providential dealings. The failure of their argument apparently leaves the divine proceedings open to criticism and without any adequate vindication. They aimed to show Job that he had no right to complain about the sufferings which God had sent upon him or permitted to befall him. But they were not successful, for Job has triumphantly maintained his ground in his controversy with his friends. But there is danger that he will imagine, or that the impression may be made on others, that he is completely right in his controversy with the providence of God. This dangerous impression needs to be corrected, both for his own sake and for the sake of those to whose instruction his great trial, and the book that records it, was designed to contribute.

In the forcefulness of his opposition to his friends, in the intensity of his inward struggles, Job has understandably fallen into expressions which cannot be approved, those in which he challenges the fairness of God's dealings. Great consideration is required when judging these expressions, and in estimating their real meaning in light of the circumstances in which they were spoken. Words wrung from him in the bitterness of his heart, and in the tumult of his feelings under the terrible pressure of his sorrows and the exasperating treatment of his friends, are not to be regarded as though they had been spoken in calmer moments. But if Job had gone no further astray than this, that in his desperation he had occasionally let slip what he subsequently regretted, and what did not express his real state of mind, no correction might have been needed.

The fact, however, is that Job was involved in an irreconcilable conflict with himself. He was in a dilemma from which he could not by his own skill or power be relieved. On the one side he was conscious of his own integrity. He knew from the testimony of his own conscience that he was not a gross and wicked offender. But how, then, can he maintain his confidence in the justice and rectitude of God in His providential government? A God who lets the wicked triumph and who afflicts the just, how can He be a righteous and a holy God? Job cannot put these two things together, though he holds them both and will not abandon either. And yet, in the honest frankness of his soul, he does not and cannot shut his eyes to the fact that they do seem to clash. Being an honest searcher, he says what he feels.

His controversy with God's providence is not therefore limited to a few passionate outbursts, which in moments of reflection he would gladly recall. But it is forced upon him by an inward necessity which he cannot escape. He still holds to his own integrity, but he also holds with an unslackened grasp to his confidence in God's righteousness. The righteousness of God shall shine forth radiantly hereafter, but why is it so strangely obscured now? This Job cannot answer. And, though his trust abides in God's ultimate justice, it is after all a trust in a God who has hidden himself.

A glimpse into one design, at least, of this infliction has been given to the readers of the book at the beginning in what is said there of the agency of Satan in bringing it about. Satan fiendishly plots the ruin of Job, laying snares which he confidently boasts will overthrow this godly man, bringing him to renounce the service of his Maker. The Lord permits the tempter to try his arts to the fullest extent. The result is his complete defeat. For Job holds fast his trust in God and succeeds in trampling the temptation under foot. And so it will always be whenever the malice of evil spirits and the rage of wicked men are allowed to assail 'the saints of God.' God's martyrs, suffering for their attachment to their blessed Lord, will adhere to Him in spite of all that can be turned against them—they will be true in order to illustrate the reality of faith. They will glorify God out of the midst of the fires.

But what did the Lord intend by permitting Satan to bury Job under affliction? This has not yet been stated. There was, of course, a plan. It cannot have been to gratify Satan, nor did God need such a test to satisfy Himself of the reality of Job's faith. Nor can we suppose that God would have allowed such overwhelming distresses to befall His faithful servant merely to convince Satan that his malicious suggestion was false. The Lord must have had a purpose which directly affected Job himself. God would not have made Job suffer as a mere spectacle for others, when there was no end to be answered affecting himself. God must have intended some good toward Job in permitting him to suffer as he did.

Some inkling of the divine purpose may be gathered from what has taken place thus far. We have already seen how triumphantly Job bore the severe and searching test applied to him. We may be sure that the desperate struggle through which he passed has developed and strengthened his faith. Job has learned to maintain his faith under new and most difficult circumstances. He has risen to a loftier exercise of faith than ever before. With no external props and aids, and in the face of all the suggestions of outward sense, he was obliged to maintain himself by the simple putting forth of faith in the unseen God. His faith could not but gather strength and clearness by the effort. When he learned to say with such confidence, *"I know that my Redeemer lives,"* in spite of all that had conspired to kill his hopes and quench his trust, there was a positive and decided spiritual gain. He was lifted to a higher spiritual sphere by all that had gone before.

An important development associated with or growing out of this new increase of Job's faith is the fresh enlargement of his spiritual perceptions. In groping eagerly about for something to lean upon, for something to support his soul in this time of deep distress, he grasps the firm pillar of his immortality and puts it into a connection previously unknown or unthought of with his present needs. A new element of truth is won in the struggle, a new ground for the tempted to stand upon, a wellspring of consolation to thirsty, fainting souls.

The Lord's plan for Job is fundamentally the same as with all His spiritual children. God desires his children to be pure and holy. Therefore, in the Lord's economy of things, He places greater concern on the spiritual welfare of His children rather than prioritizing their temporal happiness. In this regard, it is necessary for us to understand that a Holy God is willing to chasten His own children in the interest of promoting their holiness and purity. All of this action is consistent with

God's eternal love for the souls of His people. The Scriptures admonish each believer to not despise the chastening of the Almighty.

Still, though we may gather something by inference respecting the design of God in this mysterious and clouded providence, we feel the need of some authoritative disclosure of this design. We feel this need likewise and particularly for Job's sake, and for those who are to be instructed by his example. We desire this so the question raised between him and his friends should be at rest, that the truth should be distinctly stated which they have both vainly tried to discover, and so the antagonistic principles in Job's soul could be calmed. Ultimately, we desire that the righteousness of God should find a satisfactory vindication.

The explanation of the perplexed problem is given partly by Elihu and partly by God Himself. Elihu, who here appears for the first time, and whose descent is somewhat particularly described, and his motive for speaking as well, first addresses Job in a series of chapters. He pauses at intervals apparently for the sake of giving Job an opportunity to reply. Job, however, says nothing. Then the Lord speaks to Job out of the whirlwind and finally brings the whole matter to an end by restoring Job to more than his former prosperity.

No portion of this book has proved more embarrassing than the discourse of Elihu. And there is not such a great diversity of views in regard to any other portion. From early times, there has been a wide divergence of opinion as to the part God assigned Elihu—or why he is introduced at all. There has been confusion as to what relation Elihu's answers have to the mystery of Job's affliction, or what the relation of his speech is to that by the Lord. The perplexity is increased by the difficulty on the one hand of harmonizing what Elihu says with the lessons to be drawn from the discourse of the Lord; and on the other hand, of discriminating in a clear and satisfactory manner between the sentiments expressed by Elihu and those which had been previously advanced by Job's three friends.

Many have concluded that the lessons taught by Elihu and the Lord are hopelessly at variance, while the doctrine of Elihu and the three friends are identical. Consequently, they say, Elihu contributes nothing toward the true and proper settlement of the question at issue. His solution of the enigmas of Providence is alleged to be similar to Eliphaz and his associates, and accordingly open to the same condemnation—and they are set aside by the subsequent decision rendered by the Lord Himself, which is alone to be accepted as the true solution. On this hypothesis Job does not reply to Elihu because he really advances nothing new. And the Lord makes no allusion to him because he is a mere intruder who has said nothing deserving of special regard. Moreover, they say, Elihu is involved in the censure passed upon the friends, whose tenets he had simply repeated.

Among those who hold this view there is still a difference of opinion as to the ability displayed by Elihu in the presentation of his argument. Some say he is a shallow pretender, a vain upstart intruding his opinions where wiser and better men had already spoken. Others concede that his several points are made with skill and logic. They consider his speech as representing the highest results attainable without immediate divine revelation. God alone, they say, can give the correct answer where the wisest of men are incompetent to discover the truth. Elihu's failure then makes it necessary for the Lord himself to intervene.

However, it is highly improbable that so much space in the divine Word would be devoted to Elihu if he really contributes nothing, only repeating what Job's friends had said before. The difficulties which have been felt with regard to Elihu will disappear, and the hypotheses above will vanish upon a more careful study of the speech, together with close attention to the language with which he is introduced. It is plain that the writer of the book does not regard him as siding with the friends. He represents him as equally displeased with both contending parties: *"His wrath was aroused against Job because he justified himself rather than God. Also against his three friends his wrath was aroused, because they had found no answer and yet had condemned Job"* (Job 32:2, 3). Elihu then steps forth as an mediator, putting the question at issue upon entirely new ground. He does agree with the friends in some of their positions, which as general statements were quite correct. But his fundamental teaching is totally different from theirs.

Elihu is not spoken of in the beginning of the book, when the arrival of the three friends is mentioned, because there was no occasion for speaking of him then. He only engages in the dispute because the three friends have failed to find a satisfactory answer to Job. To speak of him in the outset would have been to anticipate their incapacity to deal with the subject before they had made the attempt. Job does not answer Elihu because he is convinced of the truth of what he says, and therefore he has nothing to reply.

The Lord makes no allusion to Elihu because he was not one of the parties to the strife which was to be adjusted. He was not one of the contestants, but a concerned bystander whose decision was preliminary to the Lord's. The infinite God could not in dignity place Himself on a level with his dependent creature by entering into an argument with him in justification of His own sovereign acts. Therefore, as far as there was any occasion for arguing the case with Job to correct his misapprehensions, or to vindicate the divine proceedings, this was committed to Elihu, who could meet Job as an equal. This course was also really best for Job. There was no divine terror to appall him, no power of the infinite Majesty to overwhelm him. Job could stand on a par with Elihu, God's messenger, and could make reply without irreverence if the considerations presented did not convince him. Elihu's arguments were convincing; therefore Job yielded to his arguments and did not reply. He passively acknowledges the justice of all that Elihu says. His false views are corrected and his misconceptions of God's providences and plan in sending affliction upon him are removed. The way is thus prepared for the Lord to appear, and by the simple majesty of His divine perfections, to make the needed impression on the heart of Job. The awe-struck patriarch bows at once in submissive penitence, for he has learned from Elihu to see in God no longer the impersonation of arbitrary power yielded for his destruction, but the God of grace, in whose hand even the rod of affliction was a means of blessing.

It appears that Elihu had been present during the discussion, though not spoken of before. He had said nothing, maintaining a respectful silence. This suggests the probability of the presence of others likewise. The fame of the patriarch's sorrows had gone far and wide. And as all his relatives and acquaintances came to him after his restoration, so doubtless they did while his sorrows lasted. Eliphaz, Bildad and Zophar were the spokesmen to whom the rest deferred as their superiors in age and in reputed wisdom. But the friends had shown themselves unable to still Job's complaint or to answer his arguments. They defended God's providence by discrediting Job's character. So far it might appear as though Job's complaints were justified. Upon the principles of his friends, God was treating him as though he were guilty of offenses which he had not committed. The mystery of God's providence was still unsolved. Elihu had waited, expecting the three friends to bring out the true moral reasons of the distresses that befall good men like Job, and to show the harmony of the perfections of God with His providential government. When they failed, he was irresistibly impelled to speak.

Elihu begins with an apology for speaking, which may seem repetitious. But this arises from the inexperience of speaking in the presence of the aged and wise. Yet he felt constrained to declare the truth which had not thus far been mentioned, to return the proper answer to Job. He promises that he shall be perfectly impartial, without respect of persons and without flattery. He proposes to put the matter on an entirely new basis, one altogether different from that on which it had been placed by the friends, (Job 32:14).

That which chiefly distressed Job was that God seemed to be treating him as an enemy. He had dwelt most pathetically on this and had recited his dreadful sorrows as so many evidences of the fierceness of God's anger and the bitterness of His hostility. It is to this error that Elihu first addresses himself. He says that affliction is not a token of God's displeasure but one of the measures of His grace. It is not sent in wrath, but with a kind and merciful design. It is one of the ways in which God draws men from sin and promotes their welfare.

God employs two principal methods in detaching men from wrong, in establishing them in what is pure and good. He uses His word and His providence. God's word is described in terms appropriate to the period when Job lived, prior to a written revelation, and allusive to one of the most usual forms in which immediate divine communications were then made (Job 33:15-17), *"In a dream, in a vision of the night, when deep sleep falls upon men, while slumbering on their beds, Then He opens the ears of men, and seals their instruction. In order to turn man from his deed, And conceal pride from man,"* By these sacred instructions He saves him from sin and from its punishment, *"He keeps back his soul from the Pit, and his life from perishing by the sword"* (Job 33:18). He goes on to say that God uses affliction for the same gracious end. He sends sickness and suffering to recall men to the path of uprightness. And then if the sufferer recognizes this merciful intent of his sorrows, and yields himself up to it, his pains will be removed. Their whole design will be accomplished.

This is an entirely new doctrine and exhibits the matter under a totally different aspect. The friends have seen in suffering nothing but the punishment of sin, and the displeasure of God against it. Job sees it as an arbitrary infliction, irrespective of men's desires. But the idea of a gracious purpose in earthly distresses, the idea that they show God's goodness and love, that they are meant to accomplish a kindly end, had not dawned upon any of them. Eliphaz did in his first speech approach it, using expressions similar to Elihu's, so that a hasty and superficial examination might pronounce their teachings identical. Eliphaz is saying that the man God corrects is blessed, and he tells Job not to despise the chastening of the Almighty (Job 5:18), *"For He bruises, but He binds up; He wounds, but His hands make whole."* This looks to the possibility of good results following upon affliction, which may so far counterbalance the evil that he may be pronounced happy who endures it. And God who now sends sorrow may hereafter send joy. Suffering is to Eliphaz in its proper nature punitive, and it represents God's displeasure against sin. Suffering to Elihu is productive, and it represents God's affectionate concern for the true welfare of the sufferer. The two ideas are as far apart as the poles. The development of the doctrine of the friends led directly to their gross and unfounded charges of hypocrisy and guilt. Elihu's teaching is perfectly consistent with Job's true character as affirmed by God Himself. And it quite disarms Job by showing that he has been neither unkindly nor unjustly treated. God is not treating him as a foe or a criminal, but He is showing a deliberate regard for his highest good.

The suggestion of Elihu as to the divine purpose in suffering also adds to that which is stated in the opening of the book as the occasion of the sorrows of Job. But it is not inconsistent with it, nor is it excluded by it. Though it was permitted at the instigation of Satan, who sought Job's hurt, it does not follow that the Lord had no plan of His own. Undoubtedly one design of God was to exhibit the reality of Job's faith, and its adequacy to bear the test, terrible as it was, which Satan proposed. But nothing obliges us to believe that God's merciful purpose was simply commensurate with the mischievous intention of Satan, or that it was limited to the defeating of the harm concocted against Job. Why may He not likewise have had positive designs of good, which Satan's malice was by overruling grace to be made the instrument of effecting? Elihu declares this to be God's plan. And we have already seen good coming to Job out of this seeming evil. Job has been purified and, besides being instructed, his faith is strengthened. Therefore the teaching of Elihu doesn't conflict with the rest of the book, it finds in it ample justification and support. It was the purpose of God from the first to bless Job by means of this trial. And although this purpose has not been previously announced, it is already gradually working itself out.

Job was not told that he was being put on trial, for it was not the truth he needed. But now that he has successfully borne the test, he needs to know why he was afflicted—not so far as Satan was concerned, but its end for himself. He needs to know that it was sent out of God's love, and that it enclosed a real benefit. It was necessary that he should understand this in order that he might be thoroughly released from Satan's snare, and so that he might receive the full profit that was in store for him.

Elihu's doctrine of suffering is not hampered by the rigid and inflexible rule of exact retributive justice maintained by the friends. Nor does it conflict with the general facts of Providence or with the consciousness of Job. Job's arguments against the friends do not lie against it. In fact, Job has no opportunity to argue against this view. It gives a satisfactory account of the inequalities of human conduct and consequences. The unbending rule of strict justice would have required a uniform and precise relationship between men's fortunes and their characters. The divine retribution might be postponed, but it must never fail to be uniformly poured out to all, in the true proportion of their merits and demerits.

But a gracious purpose is from its very nature free. It cannot be bound by any rule but the attitude and will of Him who exercises it. The only limitation upon God's overt act of kindness is God's good pleasure. No one can dictate in advance where He shall send joy or sorrow. In regard to God's spiritual children, He cannot love them more than He already does and will not love them less on any given day. He may by His goodness lead men to repentance. He may use chastisement to wean them from the love of this world or to turn their hearts from sin. The method He uses in each particular instance depends solely upon His sovereign will. This allows all the free variety found in the actual experience of men, while at the same time it neither divorces the world from God nor represents His dealings as arbitrary. He governs in all the affairs of men, and He does so in a manner worthy of Himself. There is a method in all that occurs, and a purpose and a divine intelligence. God's providence becomes in fact the expression, the visible manifestation of God's holiness as well as of His grace. For it is directed with the view of reclaiming men from sin and training them in holiness and virtue. It is not driven by any formal mechanical rule, nor is it designed to merely re-act to the actions of men. It is wisely adapted to fulfill the desires of Him whose resources are endless and whose understanding is without limits.

This doctrine likewise supplies the undiscovered key to the mystery of Job's sufferings. No reflection is cast on his integrity or on the genuineness of his faith. His afflictions are neither an indication of the Lord's displeasure nor of His deliberate hostility. A gracious God is by this severity of discipline purging away the dross which still adhered to His faithful servant, and refining the gold to a higher measure of purity.

Accordingly, when Elihu pauses in his discourse (Job 33:32) to give Job an opportunity for reply, he makes none. He has nothing to say in opposition to what he has heard. It has brought conviction in his soul. It has composed the strife which previously agitated him. It has reconciled the seeming contradictions. It harmonizes his convictions respecting God with what has until now been hidden in His providence. It makes all plain in his own case, where before it was dark and impenetrable. God has not been harassing Job by these terrible sufferings which He has inflicted or permitted. God has not been charging upon him a guilt of which the testimony of his own conscience acquits him. There is no hostile intent on the part of God: all has been done in kindness and in love. The truth of Elihu's testimony finds its way to Job's heart. It finds a prompt echo in Job's heart and he bows in quiet submission to the force of what has been said. Elihu has not only gained his ear, but his heart. And the solution of the mystery which has so baffled and perplexed him begins to open before him.

Having established this main position, Elihu proceeds to comment on some of Job's ill-considered and hasty speeches, which had fallen from him in the heat of his controversy with his friends. They were regularly representing God's justice as being hopelessly at war with the idea of the integrity of Job. Not seeing, in the desperate gloom that enveloped Him, how this conclusion was to be escaped, Job boldly admits it, and in the thorough consciousness of his own rectitude is driven to affirm that God has done him wrong. But now that this antagonism has been done away by the new principle which Elihu has announced, Job is no longer under any temptation to dispute the righteousness of God's providential administration. Elihu accordingly holds up before him some of his most extreme statements, pointing out their absurdity and impropriety. When Job said, *"God has taken away my justice,"* (Job 27:2) he was flirting with wicked men and dishonoring the foundations of God's universal government by claiming God has deprived him of his rights. Shall not the Judge of all the earth do right? It is repugnant to every notion of right to charge the supreme and all-perfect Ruler with injustice. If a conflict arises between God and His creatures, whom He can be under no possible temptation to injure, the overwhelming presumption is that He is right and they are wrong, whether they can see it to be so or not! *"For has anyone said to God, 'I have borne chastening; I will offend no more; Teach me what I do not see; If I have done iniquity, I will do no more?'"* (Job 34:31, 32). And he adds, *"Do you think this to be right? Do you say, 'My righteousness is more than God's?'* " (Job 35:2).

Job had consistently resented such language from his friends. Their appeals to God's righteousness always exasperated him, for the necessary implication from it, as presented by them was that he was a guilty man who deserved all that he suffered. He was indignant at these unjust assumptions and indirect reproaches. But in the mouth of Elihu there is no hidden dagger, no foolish insinuations. The simple truth of the perfection of the ever-blessed God stands alone before him in its innate majesty, free from all distortions or false conclusions. Job cannot oppose what is so self-evident. He bows in silent agreement.

Having corrected Job's errors and reproved the rash speeches into which he had been betrayed, Elihu reverts again to his fundamental principle of the design of suffering, making special application of it to the case of Job, basing it upon a faithful admonition (Job 36). He repeats: Afflictions are sent upon the righteous for their good, and this experience is alive with solemn responsibility to the afflicted themselves. If they recognize the gracious purpose of God in their sorrows and heed the lesson they involve, then the design of this painful experience will be accomplished—and it will be itself removed. If, on the contrary, they disregard the voice of love and warning which speaks to them in these distresses, they will incur the divine displeasure and bring God's judgment on themselves in the form of still heavier sorrows than they have yet experienced. So, Elihu tells Job, it will be with him. He might have found deliverance already if he had profited sufficiently by the teachings of his sad calamities and had learned from them to be more diligent in avoiding sin and had learned to cleave more unreservedly to the service of the Lord.

Elihu has now fulfilled the task assigned to him. He was charged with removing misapprehensions from Job's mind, and correcting the mistakes into which he had fallen. But it was not given to him to pull Job entirely out of Satan's snare, and to accomplish for him the full and blessed effects of his trial. This work the Lord reserved for Himself, to be performed by Him in His own person. Elihu is but His messenger sent before His face to prepare His way before Him. And now even while he is speaking, the rumbling is heard of distant thunder (Job 37:2). Heavy masses of cloud begin to darken the sky, and the advancing tempest signals the Lord's approach. Elihu points to these signs of the divine Majesty as they steadily draw near, and his own voice is hushed in awe. All are silent in solemn expectation. It is the LORD who comes.

CHAPTER 8: COMPREHENSION QUESTIONS

Elihu

1. Had Job's three friends finished their arguments before Elihu began to speak?

2. Why does the author believe that it was necessary for Elihu, or someone, to seek to straighten out some of Job's thinking?

3. Why did the writer feel that Job had pushed his arguments to the point that he created an irreconcilable conflict with himself?

4. Read Romans 8:28. Do you agree with the author's view that God must have intended some good toward Job in permitting him to suffer as he did?

5. Which side did Elihu take during his part in the conflict? Did he side with Job, the three friends, or with God?

6. Why did the author believe that God did not decide to address Elihu directly in the closing section of Job?

7. Did Job reply directly to the statements of Elihu?

8. How did the age of Elihu compare with that of Job's three friends?

9. What explanation did Elihu provide regarding why God sometimes sends affliction to His children?

10. To what extent was Elihu able to help Job sort out his confusion and false views regarding God's providence?

Chapter 9

The Lord

"Then the LORD answered Job out of the whirlwind, and said: 'Who is this who darkens counsel by words without knowledge?' "—Job 38:1, 2

We have now come to what is beyond all comparison the most amazing portion of this wonderful book. All the discourses until now, whether of Job or of the other speakers, have been well conceived and admirably expressed. They present their profound and earnest thoughts with beauty and force. They glow with elegant and appropriate imagery. All had been well and ably spoken. But now when the Lord himself speaks to Job, His discourse is fitly marked by a grandeur and a majesty altogether unmatched before, and which is worthy of the divine Being.

It might at first appear as though the speech of the Lord had no particular relevance to the circumstances in which it was spoken. And the question might be asked, "What do these appeals to the magnificence of the works of God in nature have to do with the solution of the mysteries to which this book is devoted? How do they contribute to the explanation of the mystery that is involved in the sufferings of good men?" The fact is, the Lord's comments were not directed to the clearing up of that mystery at all. It is not God's plan to offer a vindication of His dealings with men in general, or a justification of His providence towards Job. He has no intention of placing Himself in a position where His creatures can judge His conduct. He is not amenable to them, and He does not recognize their right to be censors of Him and of His ways. The righteousness of His providence does not depend upon their perceiving or approving it. The Lord does not here stand on the defensive, nor allow it to appear as though He were in any need of being relieved from the accusations of Job. It is of little interest to Him whether feeble worms approve of His dealings or confess His dealings to be right. He puts himself in a totally different attitude and moves upon quite another plane. He is the sovereign Lord of all, accountable to no being but Himself. He does not appear to vindicate Himself, but rather to rescue Job.

Job has been exposed to the fierce assaults of Satan and has successfully withstood them. The tempter employed all his power and all his craft to bring Job to forsake the service of God, but he remained firm in his steadfastness nevertheless. The reality and the strength of Job's faith were conspicuously established from the moment he uttered his memorable statement, *"I know that My Redeemer lives."* His heroic trust in God was not destroyed by the direst calamities, nor even by the wrathful frowns that seemed to darken the face of God. Job was fully vindicated against Satan's baseless slander.

But the trial of Job was not to be terminated there. It was not the divine purpose that the trial should end with this merely negative result. Nor was it enough that he should simply receive the profit which had already accrued to him from the struggle through which he had just passed. The Lord had still larger designs of good in store for His faithful servant.

The true vindication of God's providence lies in the event. It must not be judged by the confused and tangled threads which it seems to present to the beholder while in the process of being woven, but by the completed pattern when all shall be finished. The Lord has been in no hurry to justify Himself by a premature disclosure of His plans. He has permitted things to move regularly forward and to take their appointed course. But now the time has arrived for His own intervention to bring the matter to its intended end.

Satan had been allowed to bring a double evil on Job: in his outward circumstances, then in his spiritual state. He had inflicted severe external losses and sufferings, and he had involved him in a nasty inward conflict. Job had fought this latter through victoriously, so far as it was possible for him to do from his previous standpoint in spiritual knowledge. He had risen to the noble assurance that God was his Redeemer and friend and always would be. No floods of temptation could destroy this conviction, no fierceness of Satan's assault could wrest it from him. Still the cloud and the mystery remained. A disturbing element had been introduced into the patriarch's inward experience, and it was producing anxiety and distress within him. He could not restore that unruffled state of calmness which marked his condition before his trials came. But his disturbance was not to last.

It had been a valuable discipline to Job in two respects. He had been instructed and also strengthened by the intensity of the struggle which had been forced upon him. And he had in addition been prepared to receive a further spiritual lesson: he had been made sensible of a need which he did not previously know to exist—a need for instruction and deliverance. He was now in a state of readiness to welcome a new communication from God. Satan meant to tear him away from God. But he instead opened the way for larger and fuller impartations of divine knowledge and grace. He had but prepared the way of the Lord, who was now to come to Job with a nearness and fullness never before manifested to him.

The hard discipline of Job had run its course. It had brought its full effect in preparing Job to receive the blessing which God had intended all along to be the issue of his severe trials. In answer to Satan's two challenges—the outward and temporal, the inward and spiritual—God now comes to give him benefits, both outward benefits and inward benefits.

First, the Lord produces an effect on the heart of Job. He makes such a manifestation of Himself to the sufferer's soul as brings him to the deepest humiliation for all his rash and impatient comments, and all the improper reflections he had cast upon God for His providential dealings. He had already found peace with his Maker so far as his personal relation to God was concerned. Now he is entirely passive in all the Lord's dealings—he repents of his murmurings, he surrenders his wayward resistance to the divine will. And he is amazed at himself and filled with shame that it ever could have been otherwise with him. Then the Lord restores Job's outward estate and raises it to a higher measure of prosperity than before. The whole matter is thus brought to its final issue: Job's faith is recognized, and his welfare and happiness are promoted. The latter is recorded in the delightful paragraph which concludes the book. The former is accomplished by the Lord's presence and speech.

The meaning of the Lord's comments here in its relation to Job and to the problem of the afflictions of the righteous has often been misconceived and misstated. As it is chiefly occupied with appeals to the works of God in nature, which display in such a striking manner the omnipotence of the Most High in its contrast with the impotence of man, it has been thought that the main idea advanced is the infinite exaltation and power of God. His sway is irresistible. It is vain to think of opposing omnipotence. And the lesson that some consider to be primary is that of unconditional resignation to the will of the Infinite Sovereign. Since God is almighty, His will must be submitted to. The creature must yield unresistingly to what the Creator decrees. It is worse than useless to complain or murmur. Man must bow with meek submission to any circumstance, coming from such a Source.

But submission to the inevitable is fatalism, not scriptural resignation. We have to acknowledge more than an overwhelming force. It is our heavenly Father who demands our love as well as our willing obedience. We should submit to Him, not by constraint, but with a ready mind. We may be compelled to yield subjection to irresistible power, but it will not satisfy the reason nor the sense of right. It was this, in fact, which was a main factor in the temptation of Job. His unaccountable sufferings, the baseless reasonings of his three friends, and everything in his whole situation conspired to set the Lord before him as a mechanical Being of absolute and arbitrary power who was using His omnipotence to torture and destroy him without any ground or reason. Such an almighty tyrant on the throne of the universe would indeed inspire terror, but he could not awaken confidence or love. He might break down all open opposition and stamp out the very semblance of it, but He could not compel the adoration of the heart. Job, prostrate and bleeding, protested with what he supposed to be his dying breath against the cruel wrong which he thought was being done to him. Violence, when it is inescapable, is only the more dreaded and detested on that account. God is more than almighty power, or Job would not have humbled himself before Him in cordial self-abasement. He fell prostrate before an holy and personal God, which was very different from outward compulsion.

Again it has been supposed that the burden of the Lord's discourse here is God's infinite wisdom as displayed in His works, which so far transcends our faculties, baffling the most adventurous efforts of the human understanding. These appeals to the incomprehensible marvels which everywhere abound in the world are intended, it is said, to suggest the existence of marvels equally incomprehensible in God's providence. There is a mystery in all His ways, in nature, and in the affairs of men, which no human intelligence is able to penetrate. It must be accepted as a product of the infinite reason without insisting upon knowing how or why. It is not given to man to fathom what it belongs only to the divine understanding to comprehend. The ways of God are unsearchable. Man should adore where he cannot understand and submit without question to unexplained circumstances. It would be arrogant to suppose that God's decrees could be made level to man's feeble comprehension.

There is a partial truth in this view as in the preceding. God is infinitely wise and infinitely powerful, and both of these attributes of God supply considerations which enter into and enforce godly resignation. But the lesson of the book of Job, in these its most solemn utterances from the mouth of God himself, is something more than that there is nothing that we can know, that the mystery of the sufferings of good men must remain unexplained because no explanation is possible. This would not be to set at rest troubled questionings and anxious inquiries into the principles of the divine administration, and its consistency with God's unspeakable perfections. Instead, then, of shedding any light upon this mysterious subject, the only teaching of this book would be that we must remain content with a darkness that can never, from the nature of the case, be dispelled. Instead of adding to our knowledge, it would declare that further knowledge was unattainable.

And if this were the case, why should the Lord have revealed himself to Job at all in so bold a manner? In what respect was Job helped or instructed by the manifestation of God to him, if it had no other intent than that just stated? If the discourse of the Lord, with all its rare wisdom, does not carry him beyond the point which he had already reached himself, what was the need of any immediate divine intervention? Job was profoundly sensible of the mystery of God's providence. And he had confessed it to be quite impenetrable. The wisdom that could fathom it, he had said, was *"hidden from the eyes of all living,"* and was possessed by God alone. Again, the highest wisdom to which man could attain was the fear of the Lord (Job 28:20-28). Job had learned to adhere to his confidence in God, though he could not comprehend His ways; to confess the Lord to be his Redeemer, though His providence remained an incomprehensible mystery. The lesson of the Lord's discourse must be something beyond what Job had himself already attained to.

There are two things which may supply the key to what this lesson really is. The first is the preliminary speech of Elihu, by which that of the Lord is immediately preceded. The Lord's comments are not to be separated from that of Elihu, which was the preparation for it. Elihu was sent with the theoretical, as the Lord supplies the practical solution to this great problem. He was commissioned to make the needed explanations to Job, to correct his mistakes and point out to him where he had erred. His task was to clear Job's mind of every false impression and prepare Him for the coming of the Lord, so that upon His appearance he might instantly recognize Him in His true character and feel toward Him as he should. To Job's mind his sufferings had been hostile treatment on the part of God. He could look upon them in no other light than as tokens of God's displeasure. God was dealing with him in anger. He was indeed able notwithstanding to affirm that God was his Redeemer. But Elihu opens up to him a new view of the case. He shows him that this imagined hostility is not really such. God has not been dealing hardly and cruelly with him, but has been accomplishing the purposes of His grace on Job's behalf.

This alters the whole aspect of the matter. The face of God seems no more to wear a frown. What he had thought to be the terrible seizure of a mortal foe is the powerful grasp of a friend. What he had imagined to be the deadly thrust of hostile weapons proves to be the skillful incision of the great Physician who wounds only that He may heal. The chief source of Job's agitation and distress is gone. The seeming contradiction has vanished between the actual and the ideal, between what he experienced and what he might have expected, between the God of the present and of the future, between the God who afflicts and the God who saves. God is his redeemer, not merely out of existing sorrows, or in spite of them, but in them and through them and by means of them. Faith is no longer reduced to such straits that it can barely maintain itself by looking away from the present and holding fast to the unseen future. It has a visible and tangible basis in the present itself. In these very trials which had threatened to sweep away his trust in God, that trust now finds a new and firm support—for he sees in them the clear signs of God's love.

The cloud has disappeared which for a time had hidden the bright shining of his Father's face. And now when God manifests Himself to Job, there is nothing to obscure his sense of the divine favor and loving-kindness. The distorted image of God has passed away completely and forever. Unspeakable love is restored to its true place among the perfections of the Most High. His might and greatness do not stand alone, for He is also infinite in His love. It is sufficient to point out any indication of the Lord's presence or of the grandeur of His being, to bring all the divine attributes full-orbed before the mind of Job. He sees the Lord no longer through a false medium which shuts out half His glory, but as He truly is.

The same thing appears from the effect which the Lord's speeches produce upon Job. It gives him a new and more distinct apprehension of God, a more vivid and powerful impression of His glorious nature. It was not the perception of one attribute isolated from the rest, or exalted above the rest, which led him to exclaim, *"I have heard of You by the hearing of the ear, But now my eye sees You"* (Job 42:5). All his previous conceptions of God were faint and distant compared with the intimate and thorough conviction of His exalted being which now possessed his soul. It was as that which is learned by distant report compared with that which stands revealed with the clearness and evidence of eyesight. This points to no partial, imperfect, one-sided view of God, in which certain attributes are made prominent at the expense of others, some being hidden altogether, but to a complete and true perception of God in His real character. Job's impatient utterances under the pressure of his afflictions were due to a defective apprehension of the glorious character of God. Now that he sees God as He truly is, he is abashed and confounded that he ever could have spoken as he did or indulged in such feelings as he then had.

The Lord's discourse was spoken with the aim of producing this effect upon Job and of bringing him to this humbled and repentant state of mind. The important fact, and that which is really influential in the case, is that God now manifests Himself to the soul of Job. The whole address is but the unfolding of the thought, "I am the infinite and all-perfect God." And this truth is set before his mind by a series of appeals to the grandeur of God's works, by which His perfections are so strikingly displayed in contrast with the utter insignificance of man. Job is made to feel at once who it is that is speaking to him, how completely he had stepped out of his province, and of what incredible arrogance and presumption he had been guilty in venturing to pass his judgment upon the doings of the Most High.

"Then the Lord answered Job out of the whirlwind" (Job 38:1). The clouds, to which Elihu had pointed as covering the light, had grown darker and more threatening until they nearly blotted out the day. The lightning, the thunder and the tempest in which the Lord had veiled His awful majesty had been steadily approaching and filled all hearts with dread. And now from the middle of the rushing storm comes forth a voice, the voice of Jehovah, speaking to Job: *"Who is this who darkens counsel by words without knowledge?"* (Job 38:2) Who and what is he who has been daring to obscure the wise orderings of My gracious and holy providence by the ignorant and empty reflections he has cast upon them? What is his ability, and what are his claims to act as the critic of the divine proceedings? *"Now prepare yourself like a man; I will question you, and you shall answer Me. 'Where were you when I laid the*

foundations of the earth? Tell me, if you have understanding. Who determined its measurements? Surely you know! Or who stretched the line upon it? To what were its foundations fastened? Or who laid its cornerstone, When the morning stars sang together, And all the sons of God shouted for joy? Or who shut in the sea with doors, When it burst forth and issued from the womb; When I made the clouds its garment, And thick darkness its swaddling band; When I fixed My limit for it, And set bars and doors; When I said, This far you may come, but no farther, And here your proud waves must stop! Have you commanded the morning since your days began, And caused the dawn to know its place, ... " (Job 38:3-12).

The Lord further continues His appeal to the marvels of the sea, of death and the unseen world, of light and darkness, of the snow and rain, the ice and cold, of the stars, of the various celestial changes with their terrestrial effects, of the soul of man, of the instincts, habits, and adaptations of various orders of the animate creation; and concludes with the pointed interrogation, *"Shall the one who contends with the Almighty correct Him? He who rebukes God, let him answer it"* (40:2).

Awestruck and abashed at his own littleness and at the absurd pretensions involved in his rash and inconsiderate complaints, Job answered the Lord, *"Behold, I am vile; What shall I answer You? I lay my hand over my mouth. Once I have spoken, but I will not answer; Yes, twice, but I will proceed no further."* (Job 40:4, 5)

The Lord then speaks once more to Job with the view of deepening the impression already made and of showing still further of what vain conceit of his own powers Job had been guilty and what unheard-of assumptions were involved in the language he had allowed himself to use. Was he prepared to assume the government of the world and to take it out of the hands of the Most High, whose administration he had ventured to judge? God challenges Him to show a power or execute deeds of judgment which would warrant these bold pretensions. *"Would you indeed annul My judgment? Would you condemn Me that you may be justified? Have you an arm like God? Or can you thunder with a voice like His? Then adorn yourself with majesty and splendor, And array yourself with glory and beauty. Disperse the rage of your wrath; Look on everyone who is proud, and humble him. Look on everyone who is proud, and bring him low; Tread down the wicked in their place. Hide them in the dust together, Bind their faces in hidden darkness. Then I will also confess to you That your own right hand can save you."* (Job 40:8-14)

So far indeed is he from being able to measure himself with God that he cannot even cope with His creatures, as he is reminded by a reference to two formidable animals, behemoth and leviathan—probably the hippopotamus and the crocodile, although it may also be speaking about the ancient dinosaurs. The full impression intended has by this time been made on Job, and he falls prostrate before the infinite God in humble submission. Convicted of his fault, he makes instant confession, *"... I have uttered what I did not understand, Things too wonderful for me, which I did not know.... I have heard of You by the hearing of the ear, But now my eye sees You. Therefore I abhor myself, and repent in dust and ashes"* (Job 42:3, 5, 6).

Job has now reached an elevation far above his former self. The depth of his humiliation is really the summit of his exaltation in holiness and in the fear and love of God. That Job now looks down upon himself as he does shows how he has been raised above what he was before. He has made a great advance beyond the fervor of that moment when, in the darkest period of his struggle, his faith looked out with more than eagle glance into the unseen and, by one mighty effort, rose superior to every temptation.

The faith, which shone out so conspicuously in that triumphant exclamation, was nevertheless defective, or the struggle would not have been so fierce, nor the triumph so hard to gain. He trusted in God, who was afflicting him, so far as steadfastly to believe and to declare that God would certainly hereafter, in the world to come, if not in this, lay aside His seeming hostility and reveal Himself as his friend. He trusted in God in spite of these afflictions, confident that He would deliver him out of them and would then be his God. But his trust in God was not such as to persuade him that in afflicting him He was still acting as his gracious God and redeemer. He was so far under the dominion of sense that there was still a region which faith had not completely penetrated. The opposition between God's present treatment of him and His loving regard for him still remained in his mind, and he did not have that implicit trust in God which could dissolve it. He had a faith which could resolutely turn its back upon the mountain of difficulty, but not one which could say to it, Be removed! Be cast into the depths of the sea and sink out of sight! Or, be dissolved in the ocean of divine love! There was still to him an apparent contradiction here, which his faith could disregard but not dismiss. A small breach still existed between God and himself, which his faith could bridge over but not close up.

Now, however, he has learned to exercise a more perfect trust in God. He now confides in Him more thoroughly than before. He can now trust God in everything, and believe that He does all things well. He has gained such a view of God and of the perfections of His being, that he now believes that the Most High cannot do anything that is out of harmony with His perfections. All that He does must be right and wise and good. Job's faith may not enable him to fathom the mysteries of God, or to solve the riddles of His providence, but he knows that God is all-perfect and all-glorious. And he has that confidence in Him which assures him that these things must be so. If He has sent affliction, this is not even a temporary interruption of His favor and love, though these are sure to shine forth again hereafter clearly and fully. Nor is it enough to say that affliction is capable of being reconciled with the divine love. It is itself a fruit of that love. God is equally loving and gracious, whether He sends affliction or prosperous abundance.

Hymn Of Thanksgiving

For the blessings of the field,
For the stores the gardens yield,
For the vine's exalted juice,
For the generous olive's use;

Flocks that whiten all the plain,
Yellow sheaves of ripened grain,
Clouds that drop their fattening dews,
Suns that temperate warmth diffuse;

All that Spring, with bounteous hand,
Scatters o'er the smiling land;
All that liberal Autumn pours
From her rich o'erflowing stores;

These to Thee, my God, we owe—
Source whence all our blessings flow!
And for these my soul shall raise
Grateful vows and solemn praise.

Yet should rising whirlwinds tear
From its stem the ripening ear,
Should the fig tree's blasted shoot
Drop her green untimely fruit—

Should the vine put forth no more,
Nor the olive yield her store,
Though the sickening flocks should fall,
And the herds desert the stall—

Should thine altered hand restrain
The early and the latter rain,
Blast each opening bud of joy,
And the rising year destroy—

Yet to Thee my soul should raise
Grateful vows and solemn praise,
And, when every blessing's flown,
Love Thee – for Thyself alone.

Anna Loetitla Barbauld

Job's afflictions have not abated yet. His terrible losses are still as great as they were, and his bodily sufferings are as grievous. But the cloud is gone. He has lost all disposition to murmur or repine. He is amazed at himself that he could ever have done so. Since the Lord has disclosed Himself to him, such a sense of the divine perfections has filled his soul and forms the basis of an absolutely unlimited confidence. The temptation is not vanquished, it simply disappears. It is not overcome by a tremendous effort; the huge mountain just sinks down to a level plain. Though the sea roared before and was troubled, he walked in the midst of its waves unharmed and dry-shod. But now, his faith has gained in strength until it has been able to bid the sea become dry land. The billows have ceased their tempestuous roll, and there is no more sea.

Job has now come to the end of the third temptation, which is the last and most fearful stage of the temptation. The struggle has been tremendous. It has been a long and a wearisome conflict, one desperately contested. But there is a glorious end. The forces of his adversary are not merely driven back, not merely routed and put to flight—they are positively annihilated! The victory is complete and final! Job's resignation and humility in the first and second stages of his affliction were sublime. How much more sublime are they now. When his property and his children were all swept away, Job still blessed the name of the Lord, mindful of the fact that the Lord had given what He now took away. Then when his own person was visited with a dreadful and seemingly incurable malady, he meekly received the evil at the hands of the Lord, still mindful of the good which He had previously bestowed. His constant trust in God rooted itself each time in the past, in the abundance of former mercies; his grateful sense of which was not effaced by all the severity of his present trials. He put his trials in the scales over against the benefits which the Lord had so bounteously conferred upon him. The bounty substantially outweighed the afflictions.

Nevertheless each infliction of hurt and loss was an opposing weight, acting with whatever force it possessed in a contrary direction from God's mercies, and to that extent detracted from his sense of the goodness and love of God. This laid him open to the temptation of Satan. And it created the possibility that if weight enough could be accumulated on the side of affliction, it might at length create an imbalance, finally turning the scales the other way. And if this takes place, Job has fallen—Satan has gained the victory. During the most terrible period of his sorrows, when Satan seemed to have summoned every influence possible to depress the scale, Job was indeed hard-pressed by his wily and unscrupulous foe. It was as much as he could do, by straining his God-given strength to the utmost, to maintain the balance on the right side. It was only by the strenuous efforts of a faith that took hold of the unseen, and laid its grasp upon the immutable attributes of God Himself, thus pinning the scale down to the everlasting Rock, that he could keep the balance on the side of God against a pressure too great for man alone to sustain.

So there was, to some extent, a foundation for Satan's malignant sneer when he asked if Job feared God for nothing. The enemy had detected a crevice in the structure of Job's faith, into which he hoped to drive a wedge that could tear it apart and bring it down crumbling into ruins. Job's sense of God's goodness rested on the benefits received from Him, instead of the divine goodness being itself the fixed foundation, and everything received from the hand of God being for that reason counted a benefit. He judged of God by his own partial and defective notion of His dealings, instead of judging of those dealings by his knowledge of God. Job had, in the fierce conflict which Satan had waged against him, been driven by sheer necessity to base his faith on the immovable Foundation, notwithstanding the darkness and confusion of mind which still rested on the mysterious subject of his sufferings. But now God's messenger of instruction, Elihu, had pointed out to him the gracious ends of affliction, and the Lord had revealed Himself to him in the true glory of His nature; the previously existing flaw in Job's faith is closed up. The perfections of God have now become his primary stronghold. Even today, God is still occupied with the task of perfecting good men.

Heaven and earth may pass away, but the perfections of God abide, for they are incapable of mutation or decay. This is the one fixed point, the basis of all certainty and of all correct judgments. It is, in mathematical phrase, the origin to which everything is to be referred, and from which everything is to be estimated. God must ever act like God. The works of Providence have their spring in the perfections of the ever-blessed God. Sense cannot discern this. But faith affirms it, and persistently adheres to it.

This is the lesson which Job has now learned. So he retracts all his murmuring words, and all that he has said which reproached his Maker. He abhors himself for having uttered them and repents in dust and ashes. He would not now ask that question, *"Shall we indeed accept good from God, and shall we not accept adversity?"* In a very real sense, there can be no evil from the hand of the Lord. Only goodness and mercy comes from Him. He no longer puts the benefits received from God in one scale and the afflictions in the other. But afflictions are now put into the same scale with the benefits—for they, too, are benefits when God sends them. Therefore, instead of tending to create a mere counter-balance, God's blessings are all weighed on the side of good. The nerve of Satan's temptation is now cut completely. Every weight goes from now on into the scale of God's goodness, and there is no possibility of disturbing the existing order. He who has learned to place his sole and undivided trust in God, and to estimate all things by the standard of His perfection, is beyond the reach of any serious attempt to detach him from the Lord's service. To such a faith Job has risen under the felt power of God's immediate presence. He is now in a perfectly impregnable position, and Satan can assail him no longer. His spiritual deliverance is complete. The Lord's purpose in permitting these dreadful sorrows is finally fully accomplished. There is no further occasion, therefore, for their continuance.

Accordingly, the Lord now removes them. And first he pronounces in Job's favor and against his friends, *"... the Lord said to Eliphaz the Temanite, 'My wrath is aroused against you and your two friends, For you have not spoken of Me what is right, as My servant Job has' "* (Job 42:7).

They had really brought God's providence into dishonor by their supposed defense of it. By covering up and ignoring its difficulties and seeming contradictions, they had cast more discredit upon it than Job did by honestly holding them up to the light. Their denial of its apparent inequalities was more untrue and more dishonoring to the divine administration than Job's bold affirmation of them. Even his most startling utterances wrung from him in his bewilderment were less reprehensible than the false statements and false inferences of the three friends. In saying that God was treating Job as a gross offender, they indirectly charge Him with injustice and cruelty to a faithful servant of His. Job's impatient outcries under his great distress were less offensive to God than these unwarrantable misrepresentations. And now the humbled and penitent Job has retracted all that he had rashly spoken, and everything is forgiven and forgotten but his present noble confession. Stricken as he was in the dust, bleeding at every pore, he had yet placed God upon the throne and had submitted without a murmur to His holy will.

The friends of Job, who had thought him an outcast from God's favor, can only be restored to that favor themselves through the intercession of their much-maligned and injured friend. Job, of course, does not withhold this intercession. He bears no malice toward them, and no resentment for all their ill-treatment. The bitterness that had sometimes broken out in his former speeches is entirely gone. He forgives them as God had forgiven him. And with this renewed evidence of the profit which he had derived from his afflictions, Job's captivity is turned and his former prosperity is renewed and doubled.

Job is now entirely extricated from Satan's snare and released from his burden of woe. And the riddle is finally solved. The explanation of the sufferings of God's dear children may be embraced with clear understanding. They afford to all people searching for God a plain test of their integrity. The very intensity of the struggle clarifies true faith and other graces, leading the reader on to clearer views of heavenly truth. These sorrows were sent on the part of God with a gracious design, and afford the occasion of His revealing Himself to chastened souls today with new fullness and power. As a consequence, they are brought nearer to Him than ever before, and their happiness and welfare are proportionately promoted.

To this the Apostle James adds his voice, *"Indeed we count them blessed who endure. You have heard of the perseverance of Job, and seen the end intended by the Lord—that the Lord is very compassionate and merciful"* (James 5: 11).

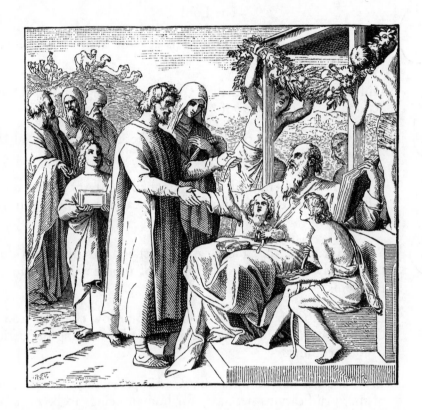

CHAPTER 9: COMPREHENSION QUESTIONS

The Lord

1. Does the Lord seek to justify His specific actions in the case involving Job?

2. Did the author believe that God was willing to subject his actions to the judgment of human creatures?

3. Why did the author think that God choose to intervene at the end of the story of Job?

4. What primary theme did God present to contrast the enormous difference between an omnipotent Creator and puny human creatures?

5. What did the author mean when he stated that the Lord does not merely bless His people inspite of problems, but through problems?

6. Did the author believe that God had somehow changed from a God of harshness and justice to a God of love during the period of Job's conflict?

7. In what sense do you think that God is providing Job with a list of the qualifications necessary for human beings to be on a par with the Lord of Creation?

8. What did the author mean when he said that the cloud had been lifted from Job when the Lord spoke to him?

9. What type of actions did God take at the end of the book of Job?

10. Why do you think that God required Job to pray for his friends before he could himself be blessed?

11. How did Job hear the voice of God compared to Jacob and Elijah? Moses?

(handwritten left margin: Did God Confuse Job with Oyer Zenemy?)

116

Chapter 10

The Book of Job in the Plan of Holy Scripture

"Blessed are those who mourn, For they shall be comforted."—*Matthew* 5:4

Having made our way through the book of Job, it is proper for us not only to form the right estimate of the book itself, but also to learn where God intended to lead us. Germs of truth are planted here, truths which God intended to expand in other parts of Scripture. The points of thought which are started here lead on to far-reaching consequences. This precious tide of knowledge flows on with ever-deepening current, gathering fresh tributaries as it flows, until we come within view of the gospel of Jesus Christ.

No book of the Bible stands apart by itself. None can be fully understood when studied separately and in its isolation. It is part of God's gradually unfolded revelation. Every book of the Bible belongs to a well-ordered system. It is a link in a chain. The history of Job is one among a great body of important facts illustrative of God's ways with men, one of many intended to reveal His plan of grace. The book of Job is one of a long series of inspired writings through which it has pleased God to make known his will and to reveal Himself. What precise part does it take in the successive disclosures of the truth of God? How does it advance upon what had been made known before? How does it prepare for what was to follow? What educating power lay in the truths which it lodged in the minds and hearts of men? And how do its teachings stand related to the completed revelation of the gospel?

It would be impossible to treat such a theme as this exhaustively within the narrow limits to which we must confine ourselves. And the attempt to do so under any circumstances might savor of arrogance and presumption. It will be sufficient, we trust, to consider a few observations by way of brief commentary.

In logical order as in actual fact, the law precedes the gospel. It is so in the experience of the race of man as a whole, in that of the chosen people, and in that of individual men. The covenant of works goes before the covenant of grace. The sentence upon our transgressing first parents preceded the promise of Him who should bruise the serpent's head. The commandments given by Moses must go before the grace and truth that came through Jesus Christ. The conviction of sin must come before the apprehension of saving mercy. Unless the lesson of the just desert of sin and of the inflexible righteousness of God has been first learned, the necessity and value of the offer of salvation cannot be understood. The doctrine of retribution is a necessary prerequisite to that of delivering grace. God must be seen as a Lawgiver and a Judge before He can be known as a Redeemer.

Paul described the Old Testament canon on occasion as "the law" (Rom. 3:19a, 1 Cor. 14:21), and was not averse to contrasting the New Covenant, with which the New Testament is chiefly concerned, with the Old Covenant. They are so contrasted by the apostle in respect to their tendencies on the whole, as the letter that kills and the spirit that gives life (2 Cor. 3:6). The foundations of law were laid broad and deep, strongly cemented by ages of the continued inculcation of God's essential righteousness. What is the Old Testament in its grand divisions but the Law proclaimed at Sinai, confirmed by the providential retributions of the History, devoutly meditated upon and practiced by the Psalmists and other inspired poets, and expanded and enforced by the added revelations of the Prophets? When the law had thus been established by all these concurrent methods into the minds and hearts and lives of men, then and not before was there an adequate basis on which to rear a superstructure for the revelation of God's immeasurable grace.

While, however, the two Testaments are predominantly what has just been described in general, they are not exclusively so. The people of God in every age have been saved by grace through faith. The gospel was already witnessed by the Law and the Prophets (Romans 3:21), and the faith of Christ fulfills and establishes the Law (Romans 3:31). Coupled with the revelation of God's justice under the Old Testament, there was a co-ordinate disclosure of His grace. For grace was set forth with growing clearness and fullness from the beginning to the end. Every advance in the presentation of the one was attended or followed by a corresponding advance in the knowledge of the other. Judgment and mercy both meet in the gospel, being reverse sides of the excellence of God. The whole of Scripture teaches us that God has unique and complementary purposes for His law and grace.

While, however, the gospel was already substantially preached before Christ came, this was primarily done in a legal form and under legal aspects. The pardon of sin, for instance, and reconciliation with God were accomplished by various sacrifices. It is true that these prefigured the atonement of the Son of God and derived from it all their ultimate meaning. Nevertheless they were a ceremonial institution, enacted in the law, to be performed by the offerer himself and making up a part of his righteousness in view of the law. Mercy came to him indeed as unmerited grace to an offender, and yet under the form of an acceptance or justification obtained by a performance of his own, or an act in whose performance he took part. The mercy that cancels sin did not drop out of sight, but it could not stand forth so conspicuously in comparison to the suffering of Christ. The shadows of Old Testament sacrifices have been merged into and superseded by the great reality, and our entire pardon and justifying righteousness are seen to be worked out by another in our stead.

And so long as the free grace of the gospel was not yet exhibited in its fullness, it was also impossible that the law itself, to which the former dispensation was mainly devoted, should attain its complete expression. Dark and threatening as Sinai was, the law never appeared in such majesty and never exerted such a constraining power on men's hearts, as when it was revealed in the transaction on Calvary.

We must now inquire into the particular function assigned to the book of Job in unfolding this blended revelation of law and gospel. One obvious characteristic belonging to the book of Job in common with the other poetical books, and in which it stands in marked contrast with the rest of the Old Testament, is that it is occupied with what is individual and personal. The books of Moses contain God's covenant with Israel as a nation. The historical books record His dealings with the people as such. The books of the prophets make known His will to Israel and concerning Israel as the people of God. These set forth the general principles and methods of God's administration. The promises and threatenings concern the entire body of the people, or some considerable section of them, and individuals share the fortunes of the mass. If prosperous abundance is sent upon an obedient people, the wicked among them participate in the abundance. If a nation of transgressors is led into captivity, the calamity involves the righteous along with the rest. But Job stands alone and by himself. He is dealt with as an individual, not as one of a certain race or nation. Particularly, he is not dealt with as one of a covenant nation, for he did not belong to such. In his history we see the righteousness of God in its relations not to Israel, but to a single man.

The Psalms record the devout meditations and aspirations of godly souls, taking as their theme God's attributes, His word or His works. The Song of Solomon, which celebrates the divine institution of marriage, forms a striking parallel to the forty-fifth psalm. Lamentations is properly an appendix to the book of Jeremiah. Leaving these out of view for the present, the three poetical books are occupied with the righteousness of God as verified in the experience of men. Proverbs exhibits this verification as a fact of ordinary observation. On the whole, and as a general rule, and agreeable to the native tendencies of things, virtue is rewarded and vice is punished. But general rules have their exceptions. And to the common order of Providence as exhibited in Proverbs there are two apparent exceptions. These are so serious in their character, yet of so frequent occurrence, that they simply demand attention. There may be prosperity without piety, and there may be piety without prosperity! The first of these is treated in the book of Ecclesiastes. It presents the case of a man of the rarest wisdom, and with every facility that abundant wealth and royal station could supply, who set himself with deliberate purpose to extract gratification from all earthly sources—but he concluded that everything was vanity. And after the baffling experiments of a lifetime, he at length came to the conclusion that the only way to secure real enjoyment and true personal welfare was through the fear of God and the keeping of His commandments.

The other exception furnishes its theme to the book of Job. This deals with the case of piety without prosperity, or the righteousness of God as exercised toward faithful sufferers. Its lessons all grow out of this theme, or cluster about it. It is here, therefore, that we are to look for that unfolding of doctrine which belongs to it in the system of the Old Testament. The righteousness of God in its more general and obvious manifestations is assumed as the starting-point. This is taken for granted as well as understood and agreed on between Job and his friends at the outset. But a crisis occurs in Job's spiritual history in which the opinions that they have hitherto entertained are not adequate. A state of affairs arises at variance with their defective notions of the divine righteousness. In the struggle that now ensues, new light is imparted and more accurate conceptions are reached. The righteousness of God had been inadequately understood in two respects, belonging severally to the two poles of Old Testament truth (or, the two phases of Old Testament instruction), the law and the gospel. The question that agitates the soul of Job is that of his personal relationship to God. Is he the object of God's displeasure, or will God accomplish his salvation? But in fact he knew neither the extent of the divine displeasure nor the greatness of God's salvation. The righteousness of God condemned more in him than he suspected, while that which he looked upon as a sentence of condemnation was a measure of God's grace.

The new impressions which Job gains of the extent and spirituality of the law of God appears from his altered language respecting himself. His oft-repeated assertions of his righteousness, which were even carried to the extent of chiding with God as having done him wrong in sending afflictions upon him which he had not deserved, are superseded by penitent confession and self-abhorrence, "*... I abhor myself, and repent in dust and ashes*" (Job 42:6). The change was wrought in his mind by the instruction received from Elihu, coupled with the manifestation of God as personal instructor. Elihu took the stumbling-block which had led to his previous false conclusions out of his way by showing Him that, in inflicting extraordinary sufferings upon him, God was not thereby charging him with unusual guilt. This cause of offense being removed, Job could listen with unprejudiced ear to Elihu's interpretation, that there was a deeper and more spiritual view of the nature of sin, as not merely consisting in actual transgressions such as the friends had linked with God's judgments, but as represented likewise in pride of heart and evil purpose (Job 33:17). With his thoughts thus turned inward, Job finds reasons for the strokes of divine chastisement which he had not previously recognized, so he cannot regard himself with the same complacency as before.

But godly men under the Old Testament nowhere reach the platform of the New in this respect, and it was impossible that they should, because the facts on which the Christian doctrine of the law and of sin is based had not then been made known. This ought to be borne in mind in estimating the language of these ancient saints. We see them maintain their own righteousness before the eyes of God when we would look rather for an humble confession of utter unworthiness. They plead with God to save them for righteousness' sake when we would expect to hear them beg instead for unmerited mercy. And we find it hard to enter into their feelings. We can scarcely acquit them of irreverence or comprehend how such good men can speak as they do.

It will afford us a partial explanation of the matter if we see that these assertions of their own goodness are mostly made in opposition to implied or open charges of criminality of which they are guiltless. The Psalmists were often, like Job, the objects of unjust accusations and slanders. And they were entitled to declare their innocence of what had been falsely alleged against them. But they do not limit themselves to the claim of being pure from that which has been wrongfully attributed to them. Old Testament believers had a much greater tendency to lay claim to an uprightness of such breadth and purity that it was open to inspection by God himself.

It is also true that in making their appeals to God's righteousness they sometimes include in context His faithfulness as well as His justice. They intend by the righteousness of God that attribute of virtue in which He does right, not merely in view of their plans, but in view of His own gracious engagements. They remember His covenant and His promises. The righteousness of God assures them that He will keep that word which He mercifully gave.

But with all these explanations we cannot but feel how differently the apostle Paul is accustomed to speak of himself, and what a different estimate he puts on his own worthiness: *"Not by works of righteousness which we have done, but according to His mercy He saved us."*— *"I am carnal, sold under sin ... The good that I will to do, I do not do; but the evil I will not to do, that I practice .... 0 wretched man that I am! Who will deliver me from this body of death?"* (Titus 3:5; Romans 7:14, 19, 24). Such an experience belongs to the New Testament exclusively. There is repentance in the Old Testament, and there are confessions of sin. There are deep views of its greatness and vileness and enormity. There are prayers for forgiveness. There are fervent breathings after greater conformity to the will of God. All the roots of the apostolic experience are there, but they are never quickened into the same intensity of life, they never reach the same expansion, they never gain that ascendancy and complete mastery of the soul which shapes all its thinking and feeling. Such excellencies as these are what makes a constant attitude of helpless unworthiness before God. Why did they not have them? Because they had never learned the lesson of the cross of Christ. The vastness of the provision first gave an idea of the greatness of the need. The sinfulness of sin was never so plainly seen as in the light of the infinite merit of the atonement which was required to erase it. And the utter worthlessness of our own righteousness first became manifest from the fact that men are justified without any worthiness or deservings of their own. Instead, they are justified by simple trust in the righteousness of Another. The full knowledge of this humbling and abasing truth altered the whole complexion of holiness. It changed the very basis of men's standing in the sight of God. Or, at least, it enabled them to see where they really did stand, more distinctly than was possible before. But this, while it banished forever all thought of any claim of merit or righteousness in the sight of God, gave a new and impregnable basis of confidence before Him, —a confidence which no craft of Satan and no storms of affliction could disturb.

It is, however, on the side of the gospel that the lessons of the book of Job chiefly lie. These are all in the direction of the more complete revelations which would subsequently be made, though they do not surpass the knowledge of God's grace which was intended for that time, nor do they ever anticipate in its fullness what was reserved for a brighter future. Piety was still *"the fear of the Lord"* (Job 28:28). The love of God had not yet been made perfect (I John 4:16, 18).

In these unfoldings of gospel truth we are not to expect any direct presentation of the person of the Messiah. He is not exhibited in the Old Testament as the personal helper of the afflicted. He is ever exhibited rather as the Hope of Israel and the Savior of the world. His coming was to introduce an era of peace and holiness and bliss. His reign was to benefit all nations, for they would flock to the mountain of the Lord, beating their swords into plowshares and learning war no more. But it was not so clear to them that this same Savior was the present deliverer of each one of His people in his own individual distress. So suffering saints in the time of their trouble are not seen calling on the name of the Messiah for help and rescue, but they call upon the name of Jehovah, unaware that they are directing their petitions to the same Person whose appearance among men shall introduce the anticipated glories of the future.

But addressing Jehovah as they do in the capacity of their covenanted Redeemer, asking of Him the help which He alone can supply, making Him the sole ground of their confidence as well as of all their affection and desire, it is in fact the Son of God to whom they make their appeal. All the knowledge they gain of this divine Savior, all the homage they learn to pay to Him, all the trust they place in Him, is a direct preparation for the doctrine of Christ. They did not know at the time that this line of instruction would converge on that other line which taught them of the Son of David and the King of Israel. The point of junction was first visibly reached when the Word was made flesh. Then the divine Redeemer and the expected Savior were consciously identified as the Lord from Heaven to whom each struggling soul had looked for deliverance, and the son of Abraham in whom all the families of the earth were to be blessed. He it was that baffled Satan's wiles and rescued Job from his snare, for He was the Seed of the woman who was to crush the serpent's head and restore the fallen race of man (Genesis 3:15).

Additional elements of Messianic instruction are found in the typical character of Job and that of Elihu. They are each representative of a class which finds its highest example in Christ. Whether the type was discerned to be such by the writer of this book and his original readers, it would be difficult to determine. But it supplies an example conformed to the model of Him who was afterwards to be revealed. It presents a character which would be better understood and appreciated when realized in Christ. And the idea to which it gives rise is certainly linked with the expected Savior in other parts of the Old Testament in a way which shows that this connection was known to the inspired penmen themselves (See 1 Peter 1:10–12).

As we suggested before, Job makes a good type of the Man of sorrows in his afflictions. This resemblance to Christ is not casual or accidental. It is a principle of divine administration that His children are made perfect through sufferings. So it was with Job. So it has been in every age. There is a difference in circumstances and in application but the principle is always the same. God's own Son, when revealed in human flesh, learned obedience by the things that He suffered (Heb. 5:8).

Elihu, on the other hand, described himself as a "messenger" (Job 33:23), an interpreter, "... *One among a thousand, To show man His uprightness....*" He had been selected from all others and sent by God to expound to Job the divine will and purpose in this dispensation and to make known to Job his duty. And this was the result which he had foreshown, *"Then He is gracious to him, and says, 'Deliver him from going down to the Pit; I have found a ransom'"* (Job 33:24). Elihu acts the part of an instructor who is the instrument of salvation to his suffering and needy friend. He fulfills in a lower sense the very function of the great Teacher and Prophet, in response to whose prevalent vindication the same reply is given, *"Deliver him from going down to the Pit; I have found a ransom."* Only the ransom is then no longer limited to the figurative sense in which Elihu uses it. The great Teacher has provided a ransom in the strict and proper sense for the release of His people, now and forever.

124

As the book of Job circles about the conflict in which this man of God was engaged, its lessons mainly concern the foe with whom he had to contend on the one hand, and the supports and encouragements given to him on the other. His real adversary was not God, as his friends alleged, and as he sometimes understood it, but Satan was his foe. And here a new view is opened into the darkness. The great foe to human peace and goodness is here for the first time in Scripture clearly disclosed in his proper person and character. The serpent had tempted Eve, yet the narrative of the Fall requires the assumption of a spiritual agent concerned in the transaction, though his agency is only vaguely inferred. Here in Job, however, he is explicitly named as Satan. His spiritual nature, his malignity, his great power, his subtlety, his untiring evil are exposed. Yet he is also shown to be limited, restrained, overruled, and under God's direction so that good may be brought out of the evil he devises. This is an important advance toward the full New Testament revelation on this subject in which a disclosure is made not merely of a single adversary, but of the whole hierarchy of evil. This awareness also provided a heightened assurance of victory over evil forces already vanquished by the Captain of our salvation.

We see in Job how his afflictions were a test of the sincerity and strength of his holiness, and how his confidence in God's righteousness carried him successfully through; how he clung to his belief, in spite of all outward appearances, that God was faithful and would not desert His servant, and how at length he learned that affliction might be converted into a benefit. Of course there is a striking difference between the demeanor of the apostles and followers of Christ under calamity and that of the saints of God in the Old Testament. The moans and complaints of desertion which are so often heard from faithful men of old in times of sore distress grow directly out of the legal aspect under which they contemplated the character of God. How different it would have been if Job and the others had read, as we do, *"He who did not spare His own Son, but delivered Him up for us all, how shall He not with Him also freely give us all things?" "Who shall separate us from the love of Christ? Shall tribulation, or distress, or persecution, or famine, or nakedness, or peril, or sword? ... Yet in all these things we are more than conquerors through Him who loved us. For I am persuaded that neither death, nor life, nor angels, nor principalities, nor powers, nor things present, nor things to come, nor height, nor depth, nor any other created thing, shall be able to separate us from the love of God which is in Christ Jesus our Lord."* (See Rom. 8:32, 35, 37-39). Surely in this consciousness Job would have gloried in tribulation, assured that he would be kept from real harm by his Heavenly Father.

Again, how differently would the saints of old, such as Job, have felt if they could have known of the heavenly inheritance, that far more exceeding and eternal weight of glory with which the sufferings of this present time are not worthy to be compared. Job was brought in his conflict into contact with the doctrine of immortality, but he only attained a limited conception of this blessed truth. He was not able to draw from it that abundant comfort which it is adapted to supply. His confidence that God would not forever withhold His favor from him, coupled with the fact that there was no room left for that favor to display itself in the present life, had driven him to the conclusion that it must be granted to him in the world to come. He laid hold of his immortality to steady himself in the absence of any earthly hope. It never occurred to him to prefer it to every earthly hope, even if this latter had been possessed in the fullest measure. Life without God's favor and blessing would not indeed have been an object of desire to him any more than to the Psalmist, who exclaims, *"Whom have I in Heaven but You? And there is none upon earth that I desire besides You"* (Ps. 73:25). But life with God's favor was his chief inheritance and his portion. The idea had not presented itself to his mind that the boundless hereafter with the blessing of God's everlasting presence was a more desirable portion than this brief life could be with the same divine presence and blessing here. He had faith that God would vindicate His servant and appear upon his side in the future state. But he did not have the full conception of a life with God, a life free from sin and every form of sorrow, a glory and bliss eternal. It was not until the divine Savior had Himself appeared, and the magnitude of redemption and its unending results had in consequence been disclosed, that men could say with the apostle Paul that though to live was Christ, yet to die was gain.

The sense of immortality to which Job attained was likewise echoed by the Psalmists, who speak upon occasion of the future life, but in ambiguous and doubtful phrases, which leaves it uncertain how clear their conceptions may have been. The prophets possessed a similar view of eternity by way of a somewhat different route. God's covenant faithfulness to Israel secured His people as a whole in all perpetuity against eternal death and destruction. And this deliverance from death and from all the evils resulting from the Fall, was pledged to each member of the covenant community in Israel who was faithful to Jehovah. Still, Old Testament believers often found the path to eternal glory somewhat cloudy and difficult to comprehend.

But these flashes of assurance which we find in the Old Testament are as nothing compared with the clear and steady light shed on the future life in the New Testament. And this fullness of revelation has revolutionized the whole idea and aim of life. The believer has learned to regard the transient present as of small account in comparison with the eternity that lies before him, to set his affections on things above, not on things on the earth, to lay up his treasure in Heaven, to look not at the things which are seen and which are temporal, but to look at the things which are not seen and which are eternal. With such a blissful portion in prospect, what are all the light, momentary sorrows we suffer now?

> *To see with my heart, to feel with my soul*
> *To be guided by a hand I cannot hold—*
> *To trust in a way that I cannot see—*
> *That's what faith must be.*
>
> Michael Card

CHAPTER 10: COMPREHENSION QUESTIONS

The Book of Job in the Plan of Holy Scripture

1. Why is it important to view each book in the Bible as part of a well-ordered system?

2. Why did the author believe that the gospel of Christ is more glorious and meaningful when it is preceded by a discussion of the law of God and man's fallen nature?

3. What did the author mean when he stated that the Book of Job presents the account of how God deals with individuals in contrast with the majority of the Old Testament which emphasizes the Lord's dealing with nations?

4. Did Job have access to a full understanding of the doctrine of God's love? Explain your answer.

5. Explain why godly men in the Old Testament were more prone to justify their own innocence before God, compared to godly people in the New Testament era?

6. Due to the fact that God requires truth in the inward part of man Why do you think that the Lord singled out a good man like Job to spiritually test?

7. It has sometimes been said that once a cross or burden is gladly accepted, it ceases to be painful. In what sense do you think this statement is true?

8. How has your study of the book of Job helped you to be better prepared to lay up for yourselves treasures in heaven?

THE END

Outline Of The Book Of Job

I.   The Prologue in Heaven: Satan's Challenge and God's Reply
      (Chapters 1-2)

      A.   From Prosperity to Woe and Tragic Loss (1)

      B.   Rejected by Society and His Own Wife, and Marred by
            Hideous Illness, Job Is Visited by Three Old Friends
            —Eliphaz, Bildad, Zophar (2)

II.   Job's Debate with the Three Counselors: The First Cycle
      (Chapters 3-14)

      A.   Job Expresses His Despair (3)

      B.   Eliphaz Kindly Protests and Urges Humble Submission
            (4)

      C.   Eliphaz Exhorts Job to Repentance (5)

      D.   Job's Remonstrance and Defense against Eliphaz (6-7)

      E.   Bildad's Rejoinder to Job: Your Sniveling Complaints
            Impugn the Justice of God and Attack the Foundation
            of the Moral Order! (8)

      F.   Job's Response to Bildad: No Mortal Man May Argue
            His Innocence before the Almighty; yet He May Protest
            against Cruelly Unfair Treatment (9-10)

      G.   Zophar's Response to Job: God Is Right and You Are
            Wrong! Better Get Right with Him, for the Wicked Are
            without Hope (11)

      H.   Job Answers His Accusers (12-14)

III. The Debate Continued: The Second Cycle (Chapters 15-21)

      A.   Eliphaz Accuses Job of Presumption in Disregarding the
            Wisdom of the Ancients and Criticizing God As Unjust
            (15)